Guide to CANADIAN VEGETABLE GARDENING

Published by Cool Springs Press
101 Forrest Crossing Boulevard, Suite 100
Franklin, Tennessee 37064

Cataloguing in Publication data submitted for approval

EAN: 978-1-59186-456-1

First Printing 2009
Printed in the United States of America
10 9 8 7 6 5 4 3 2 1

Managing Editor: Billie Brownell
Art Director: Marc Pewitt

Photography and Illustration
Zone and hardiness maps: © Her Majesty the Queen in Right of Canada, 2008
iStockphoto.com and its artists: 8, 9, 39, 43, 55, 70, 71, 73, 75, 79, 81, 83, 85, 87, 89, 91, 93, 95, 97, 99, 101, 103, 105, 107, 109, 111, 113, 115, 117, 119, 121, 123, 125, 127, 129, 131, 133, 135, 137, 139, 141, 143, 145, 147, 149, 150, 151, 153, 155, 157, 159, 161, 163, 165, 167, 169, 171, 173, 175
Thomas Eltzroth: 16, 49, 51, 57, 59, 68, 69, 77
Douglas Green: 176
Marc Pewitt: 23
Felder Rushing: 33
Neil Soderstrom: 21, 26, 36

Visit the Cool Springs Press Web site at www.coolspringspress.net.

Guide to CANADIAN VEGETABLE GARDENING

Douglas Green

COOL
SPRINGS
PRESS
Growing Successful Gardeners™
www.coolspringspress.net
FRANKLIN, TENNESSEE

Dedication

This book is for Mayo —

An heirloom garden seed expert in her own right, she shares my garden and my life, putting up both with me and my love of new hybrid plants to try out.

I can't begin to thank her enough.

— *Doug*

Contents

GARDENING IN CANADA

Vegetables, Eh?

❖

Let's get the most important stuff out of the way first. First, gardening is supposed to be fun, and secondly, it isn't rocket science.

Has To Be Fun, Right?

I've been gardening all of my adult life and I hate hard work; in fact, the entire focus of my way of gardening is to have fun and eat well without working hard at it. The only time gardening stops being "fun" is when you bite off more than you can chew and try to do things in an old-fashioned, work-intensive way. I'll give you easy tips throughout this book, but if you want to ignore them because you prefer the old-fashioned methods, well, then you're on your own.

It Isn't Rocket Science

Gardening isn't rocket science. (Or, in other words, close counts.) So when I say plant something 2 cm deep, I really mean to plant as close to that as you can. A little deeper or a little shallower isn't going to spell wrack and ruin to your backyard efforts. What you need to know to be successful is in this book. It isn't fancy and you'll surely learn something on your own every year because no one can get it all into one book. But, if you find yourself getting too obsessed with figuring out how to do something, take a deep breath and reread this paragraph.

Boring But True

Raising a good crop of vegetables starts with good soil. I know this is boring stuff but good soil is at the bottom of good plants (pun intended!). For most of us in this country, this means having to make some good soil. Unless you're one of the very lucky ones who fell into an area of great soil and climate (can you say Lower Mainland in BC or Holland Marsh in Southern Ontario?) your first-year garden won't be as good as your third-year garden and even that will pale beside your fifth-year garden yields. Check out the easy and the quick methods to improving soil on pages 21 to 30.

Resources for Canada

My experience with many small—though excellent—Canadian gardening resources is that they change *way* too often. Companies change websites, change telephone numbers, go out of business, or stop offering mail order. Compared to the elephant next door, the economics of providing mail-order operations in Canada is not overly encouraging because of our smallish population. It's not a great way to make a living (… he said, from limited personal experience with his own nursery).

Bottom line: I'm going to give you the basics of good growing. The tips in this book will work across the country but you're going to have to use the Internet to get the most up-to-date listings of mail-order resources for vegetable varieties that will grow best in your neighbourhood.

The best print resource for finding up-to-date mail-order information is using garden writer Margaret Bennet-Alder's book available from her at http://torontogardenbook.com. (Yeah, I know it says Toronto but that's where this fine lady lives and I don't hold that against her.) She updates it yearly.

The best online resource (large and searchable by province, but not updated regularly) is my buddy Donna Dawson's website resource section at www.icangarden.com.

Now, onward!

Seven Rules of Thumb to Consider Before Anything Else

I've got lots of tips and hints to share with you, but I'm putting my absolute top seven rules of thumb first in this book for a reason. This is what it's all about in vegetable gardening.

Planting. I've said that close counts, but it's better to plant shallower rather than deeper. This doesn't mean we want to create shallow relationships with all our vegetable friends, but it does mean that if you have a choice to plant seeds a little too deeply or too shallowly, then pick shallow every time.

Mulch. If you do nothing more, if you learn nothing else from this book, I hope you learn that mulch is the key in our modern soils to creating and maintaining a great garden. A 7-cm layer of mulch will reduce your weeding and work by 80 percent; a 10-cm layer will bring that labour-saving into the mid-90 percent range. And the decaying mulch adds the necessary organic matter that makes your soil better.

Organic. Modern plant research has proven organic methods create both a more nutritious vegetable crop with more vitamins and minerals and a healthier plant that is far less susceptible to insects and diseases. I also notice that more municipalities and provinces are banning the use of agricultural chemicals for home use, so learning about organic production is not only smart, it's going to be necessary.

Compost. If you want superior results, learn how to make compost and compost tea. This is not only good recycling, it's state-of-the-art research findings. The objective to adding compost to a garden is to provide the beneficial microorganisms that help our plants. Compost tea is the method we use to do this when we can't produce enough compost; a handful of good compost will produce enough compost tea and microorganisms for an acre of ground.

Taste. Not only can you can save energy and money by growing your own, but *fresh is better*. You already know this but you won't truly understand it until you've picked a cob of corn and it's cooking within one minute of being picked. You won't understand this until you've tasted celery (yes, it does have a taste), or fresh carrots, or a vine-ripened tomato sliced between two pieces of freshly buttered toast. Fresh from *your* garden is the way it's supposed to be and the way many of us have forgotten.

Selection. Have enough confidence in your taste buds to make your own plant choices. Plants that come from big garden shops and chain stores are not chosen for your region. They are centrally grown and shipped from seed that is chosen for germination rates rather than taste. You can do better yourself with a little practice and discrimination about which varieties you like or by finding a local garden shop that sells the plants that grow well for the owners. All plants are not created equal when it comes to both taste and performance; you're going to find

variability from year to year even in the same variety. If you start to obsess over which tastes best, see the first two gardening rules.

Variety. Choose the standard plants you'll eat, then add one or two "interesting" varieties every year to experiment with. Don't start with one of everything in the seed catalogue (although I know you'll ignore this advice and wind up with far too many seeds) but rather restrict yourself to things you actually eat. And yes, when you do succumb to the "just-this-one-more" siren call, seeds do last from year to year and you'll easily get three years out of most seeds if you store them in a cool and dry place.

Canadian Zone Maps and What They Mean

A zone map is a guideline to the "average" lowest and highest temperatures for a particular zone. It isn't a rule to be carved in stone. That pretty much sums it up. Zone areas are more relevant to growing perennials and woody plants than they are to growing vegetables (which primarily are annuals).

The One Important Factor

The important thing to understand is that the lower the zone number, the colder your zone is, and the shorter your growing season will be.

The shorter your growing season, the more attention you need to pay to picking the right varieties. Living in near-tropical Victoria, BC, with their zone 8 gardens, means these folks can grow a very long-season plant such as an 80-day tomato. (An "80-day" tomato means it requires 80 days to reach maturity to be harvested.) But, if you tried to grow that same 80-day tomato in Edmonton, you'd never see any fruit. Up there, a "long-season" plant is anything approaching 65 days.

To complicate things a bit, a zone map based on temperature isn't going to take into account the amount of sunshine a garden is going to get. So gardens in the Maritimes, with their fog and humid conditions, can experience a different growing season than gardens in the Prairies. The length of a growing season might be the same when it comes to frost dates, but the amount of sunshine is going to vary and that makes a difference.

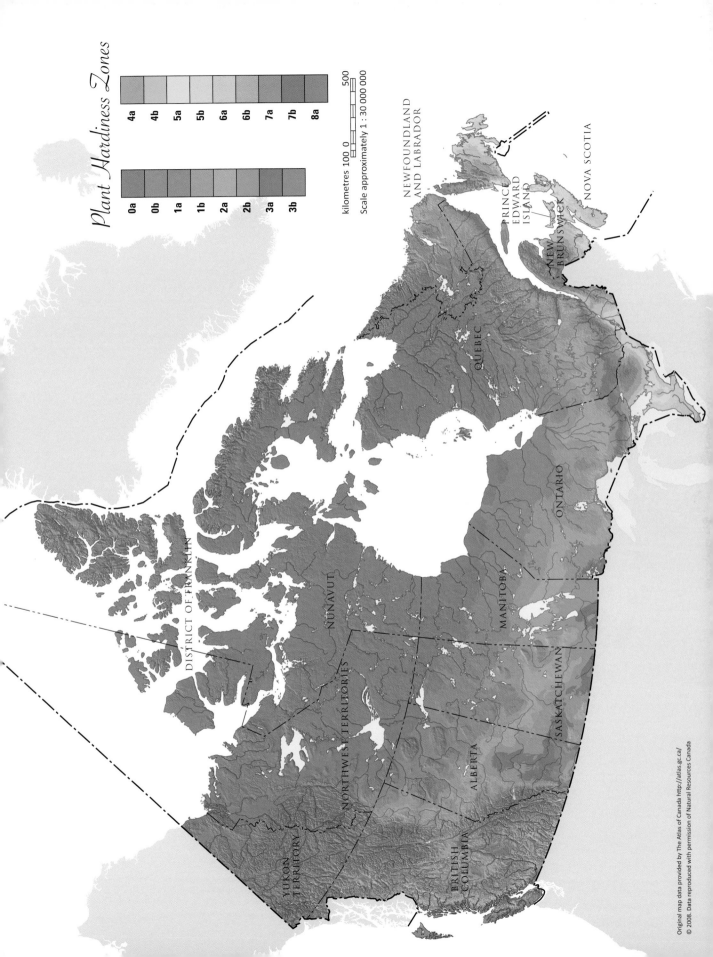

Plant Hardiness Zones

4a	0a
4b	0b
5a	1a
5b	1b
6a	2a
6b	2b
7a	3a
7b	3b
8a	

kilometres 100 0   500

Scale approximately 1 : 30 000 000

NEWFOUNDLAND AND LABRADOR

PRINCE EDWARD ISLAND

NOVA SCOTIA

NEW BRUNSWICK

QUEBEC

ONTARIO

MANITOBA

SASKATCHEWAN

ALBERTA

NUNAVUT

DISTRICT OF FRANKLIN

NORTHWEST TERRITORIES

YUKON TERRITORY

BRITISH COLUMBIA

Original map data provided by The Atlas of Canada http://atlas.gc.ca/

© 2008. Data reproduced with permission of Natural Resources Canada

Last Frost

Average Dates of Occurrence of Last Frost in Spring

April 1 April 15 May 1 May 15 June 1 June 15 July 1

© Her Majesty the Queen in Right of Canada, 2008.

NEWFOUNDLAND AND LABRADOR

PRINCE EDWARD ISLAND

NEW BRUNSWICK

NOVA SCOTIA

QUEBEC

ONTARIO

MANITOBA

SASKATCHEWAN

ALBERTA

BRITISH COLUMBIA

NUNAVUT

NORTHWEST TERRITORIES

DISTRICT OF FRANKLIN

YUKON TERRITORY

St. John's

Halifax

Quebec

Montreal

Ottawa

Toronto

Winnipeg

Regina

Edmonton

Yellowknife

Vancouver

First Frost

Average Dates of Occurrence of First Frost in Autumn

August 1   September 1   October 1   November 1

August 15   September 15   October 15

© Her Majesty the Queen in Right of Canada, 2008.

What Do You Mean By 80-day or 60-day Varieties?

Vegetables are all rated for "days to maturity" and these numbers are shown in every good seed catalogue and on the package. The ones that don't show this data tend to be the mass-merchandisers whose objective is to sell you something—but not necessarily sell you the right something.

A "day to maturity" figure depends upon the number of heat units a plant requires to ripen. This heat-unit number is translated into the number of days based on the average number of heat units in a summer's day.

You will quickly figure out that, as the weather changes (from week to week and season to season), this heat unit per day figure is going to change. If a plant requires 80

"days" to mature, it might do this in 75 calendar days one year or it might take 95 calendar days the next to produce a ripe fruit. It all depends on the weather. You get more heat units on bright, sunny days and fewer on cloudy days.

We treat the days to maturity rating as a rough guideline. In this way, a 65-day tomato will ripen before an 80-day tomato. But, the actual number of calendar days required for maturity is not a mathematical certainty.

The colder your zone, the shorter the day-length (number of hours of daylight) you want to choose when selecting specific vegetables for success. And yes, that does mean that Edmontonians aren't going to be very good at growing heat-loving plants such as long-day giant watermelon but those basking in Southern Ontario sunshine are going to have them for lunch and dinner. New-foundlanders with their fog and cool winds are similarly challenged, even though their growing season is longer than Edmonton's.

The Best Advice Is Local Advice

My best advice is to discover your local last-frost date in the spring and the first-frost date in the fall. This is a very local bit of gardening lore that area garden centre owners have engraved on the inside of their eyelids. They live and breathe this information and will share it with you for the asking. Plant and plan on harvesting within those dates. You'll see more approximate frost data on the map on pages 14 and 15.

If you decide to plant *before* this last-frost date, you take your plant's life in your hands. A late-killing frost will have you (and the other hundred gardeners in your neighbourhood) running back to the garden centre for more transplants to replace the tender ones that didn't make it. It's far better to wait a few days than to push planting by a few days. Or, use my frost-beater tips a bit further along on page 19.

And this is where the huge variation in Canadian gardening—literally, from balmy Victoria with its palm trees to Yellowknife with its late springs and early winters—creates a problem for any author. There's simply no way to suggest good varieties for every neighbourhood, but there's always somebody in each area who knows. These folks are at local garden clubs, libraries, markets, or they have the best garden in town. Ask around and you'll quickly discover who's in the know and which plants (out of thousands) are the winners.

If you're in doubt, shop at a local garden centre where they start their own plants from seed. Do not ask at a place that buys in its plants. If you're really in doubt, buy a plant that has the shortest days-to-harvest number on the tag, no matter where you shop.

Victoria Day Weekend Planting Rule of Thumb

A rule of thumb across the country is that Victoria Day Weekend is a good planting date for tender plants. You'll want to hold off a week if you're in zone 4, and two weeks if you're in a cold zone 4 or even zone 3. Those in the balmy South can cheat a week or two ahead of that date depending on the season. For everyone who lives in a zone colder than 4, wait a week to plant. For every zone warmer than 5, advance the date by a week.

Yes, I know this holiday is sometimes "early" and sometimes "late" in the month. My advice is to buy your plants on or just before the holiday weekend when the choices are still good, but don't plant them until later so the ground is warm enough to grow a good crop.

This is all common sense. If the spring has been cold and wet, then putting your plants in the ground doesn't make sense. If spring has been one glorious day after another, then get those plants into the ground. There is no hard and fast rule in this capricious land of ours.

There is a ton of when-to-plant lore on the Internet and discussed endlessly in gardening circles. The only one that ever worked for us in the nursery was to look at the long-range weather forecasts. If the forecast was clear sky with no clouds in the maybe-plant-now timeframe, we'd hold off because frosts come more often on clear skies. Those clear skies often indicated a killer frost was lurking about in early May in our zone 5 garden.

The Old Farmer Rule for Planting

There's a very old story about finding the right soil temperature for planting based on being able to sit on the bare ground with your pants around your ankles. If your bare bottom could take the cold ground, then so could your plants.

In the interests of Canadian reserve and decorum, let me suggest the inside of your wrist is equally sensitive.

If it's too cold for your wrist, then it's too cold for plants.

My Garden Is Colder Than My Zone

Yeah, it's a weird country for that. We have more microzones than we have members in the House. A microclimate is something that can either help or hurt our gardens, but here are two major tips to improve your specific garden.

Protect plants from the wind. Either create a windbreak (fencing or shrubs) or take advantage of a natural wind barrier to protect your garden. I live on an island and the wind from the southwest constantly sweeps across this chunk of land out in Lake Ontario, sending chills through tender transplants. When the wind blew down the pole bean supports, we knew it was time to move the garden behind the house.

Plant next to a large thermal barrier, if possible. If you can tuck your garden up against a large rock mass you'll find the rocks will absorb a lot of summer's heat and radiate that back to your plants in the late summer and fall evenings when they can use a little extra heat at night to keep them alive. On the other side of the ledger, that area will warm up in the spring a little later. You can build your own stonewalls, as some of my more berserker-gardening friends have done, to create an artificial heat zone.

This also assumes that you're planting in full sunshine because partial sunshine doesn't support a good vegetable garden.

Two More Thoughts on Microclimates and Pushing the Season

There are several ways to push the season along a bit earlier by creating microclimates. The first is to warm the soil for several weeks before planting. You can do this by clearing away the mulch to expose the bare soil and then laying clear plastic over that area. Weight down the edges of the plastic so wind cannot get underneath and you've created a miniature solar collector. The soil will heat up nicely in a few weeks, and you can then put tender transplants into the warmed soil.

And yes, I know the recommendation in most gardening books is to use black plastic instead of clear. The reality is that clear plastic will heat up the soil faster than black. Remove the clear plastic before planting; we want to heat up the soil in the spring, not bake the plant roots during the summer. After the plastic is removed, restore the mulch to preserve the heat, and plant.

You then have to protect the plants from cold air. This is done by making a support that looks like a mini-greenhouse out of wood or plastic pipe and laying Reemay® or another frost-protection fabric across this support. Weight the edges down for wind protection and you now have a light frost-protection system set up.

Use the plastic to heat up the soil and the mini-greenhouse concept to protect your plants and you, too, will be growing tomatoes in Bonavista. (But choose an early tomato variety, like 'Siletz' at 52 days maturity.)

Soils and Compost

The Hard Way to Improve Soil

The time-honoured way to improve soil is by double digging. Add a lot of compost or other organic matter. Rake it level. Plant and enjoy an outstanding crop yield. Double digging really works and you simply can't beat it for growing root crops such as carrots. But it's work. Hard work. You can get a sense of it in the diagramme on page 23.

Double digging. Doesn't that term just make you break out in sweat at what it might entail? I can tell you that it will make you break out in sweat before you're done with it. I only use this technique now with root crops I really want to grow (I double dig small sections of the garden for them) or for really bad soil that I want to improve instantly. It is hard work, there's no getting around this fact.

But I can also tell you that using this technique *doubled* my carrot yields. And, yes, in the old days, I did use this system on over one-half acre of perennial garden beds. And yes, it took a long time but it was worth it.

Double digging is the old (we're talking hundreds of years here) garden technique that is still as effective today as it was back in medieval Europe.

Test Double Digging

Let me suggest a simple test for you. On a small bed, follow the directions I've provided. Grow a few vegetables and a few herbs in this bed next year. Grow the same plants right beside them on a section of bed that you prepared as you've always done. See which bed produces more. (Grow carrots if you want to be amazed!)

Double digging can be used for any size bed, but I generally used a 1 by 2.4 m plot to make the project manageable and I split the work into chunks I could manage in an hour or so.

How to Double Dig

Dig a trench across the width of your garden bed 45 cm deep and approximately 30 cm wide. (The depth originally came from the instructions of "double the depth of a normal shovel's blade," hence the term *double digging*.)

The soil from this trench can be tossed to the far end of the bed. This is why I limit the length of my working bed, so I can easily toss the soil. If your version of an easy toss is less than mine, then make your working bed shorter.

You now have a trench with a pile of dirt 1 by 2.4 m away. Congratulations!

Now, dig a second trench beside the first so you have a .6 m wide trench across your garden bed.

But I don't want you to throw the soil to the end. I want you to fill the first trench in. As you dig the second to fill the first, remove all rocks, weed roots, and any other flotsam or jetsam you find. As I'm filling in my first trench, I also add compost and peat moss.

Adding Compost & Peat Moss

For every 3 shovels full of original garden soil I move, I add a shovel of peat and a shovel of compost. So the digging rhythm goes: Three shovels of

Need a quick math lesson? If you understand inches better, remember: 1 inch = 2.54 cm, so a trench about 30 cm wide is about 12 inches, or 1 foot, wide.

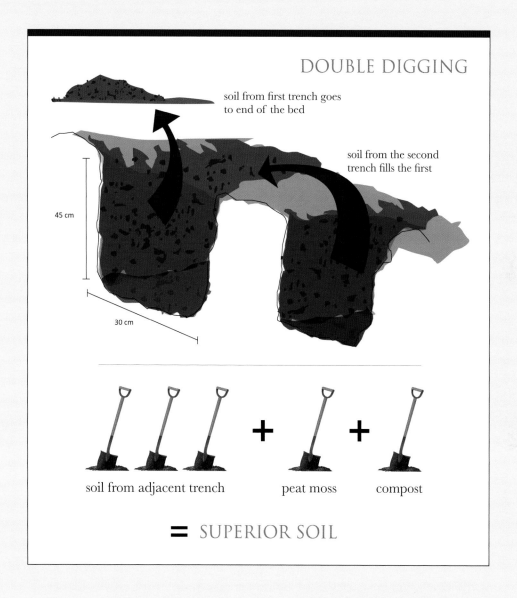

DOUBLE DIGGING

soil from first trench goes
to end of the bed

soil from the second
trench fills the first

45 cm

30 cm

soil from adjacent trench   +   peat moss   +   compost

= SUPERIOR SOIL

soil, 1 shovel of peat, 1 shovel of compost. Three shovels of soil, 1 of peat, 1 of compost. I don't bother mixing them; tossing them around seems to do the job. I do, however, try to spread the peat and compost over the soil.

I continue doing this until I have a second trench dug and the first trench filled in. The first trench is now full of a superb soil, it is well aerated, has no rocks or weeds, and is full of organic matter (peat and compost) a full 45 cm deep so new roots will have no trouble penetrating and finding nutrients.

You can see what's coming, I'm sure. Once you've finished digging the second trench (and filling in the first), it is time to dig the third trench and fill in the second.

You continue digging and filling in all the way down the garden bed until you get to the pile of soil. Use that pile of soil to fill in the last trench (don't forget the peat and compost!).

If all has gone according to plan, you now have a series of filled-in trenches and a superbly dug garden bed. The level of this aerated garden bed will be higher than the surrounding soil because of the aeration and the extra compost and peat you've added. Don't worry about it; the bed will settle out in a week or two.

Don't Walk On It!

Do not let people walk on this bed. Their weight will compact the soil and reduce all your work to a shadow of its potential.

I double dig my small kitchen and fresh herb garden every year so I have outstanding fresh vegetables for summer use. Rotating the double dug area around means that the entire garden is double dug every five years.

Double digging is not for the faint of heart. It is garden work of a serious kind but one that produces healthy plants and amazing yields.

The Noisy Way: Roto-tilling

Some gardeners decided that tilling the soil is an effective substitute for double digging and that's *almost* true. A tiller digs down about 15 to 20 cm and nicely churns up the soil.

However, the research on this style of gardening shows us that on soils with slightly higher levels of clay, the tiller is actually creating a hard-pan layer where the tines rub on the bottom of the soil. In other words, a layer of hard-packed soil is created at the bottom of the tilled soil. This will prevent some plants from growing roots past the tilled areas and it is not considered a very good thing. On sandier soils that don't compress easily, this isn't so bad as it is with clay soils, which turn solid quickly when compressed.

But on all soils, a tiller chews and cuts up the fungal strands that exist in the soil to help plants grow. This sets back the growth and health of the soil microorganisms; this in turn directly slows down the growth of plants.

So, many gardening experts no longer recommend tilling the soil with roto-tillers.

The Easy Way: Constant Mulch Gardens

This seems to be where the research is taking us for home gardening. You lay down a permanent mulch on your garden of whatever material whose appearance you like or is the least expensive.

It has to be organic in nature, so rock and plastic mulches are out. You want this to degrade.

Wood and Nitrogen

Gardeners often use bark chips and sawdust as a garden mulch. Wood products such as these are often (wrongly) pilloried as "eating up nitrogen" in the soil when you use them as a mulch.

Here's the deal in the vegetable garden. You want microorganisms to help your vegetables grow, and the ones that do the most for this kind of crop are bacteria. So you want a lot of beneficial bacteria in your soil. Bacteria thrive on organic matter that is not cellulose-based (that is, not wood).

Fungi eat cellulose (wood). So if you mix wood products into your soil, you're giving the fungi a lot of food to eat and they'll be happy. But fungi are not the microorganisms we want for vegetables.

When you give the fungi food to eat, they're going to try to hog the soil nitrogen for their purposes and take it away from the soil bacteria that we do want. It becomes a battle between the fungi and bacteria as to who is going to get nitrogen and thrive. This battle is what "ties up" the nitrogen.

So we don't want to dig in the wood chips or sawdust. We don't want to make them available to fungi for growth right through the soil where the vegetable roots are being supported by the bacteria.

But we can *mulch* with these products with no problem. The mulch stays on the surface (you don't dig it in) and there is only a very thin layer of interaction between the fungi and their food source. We still need fungi in the soil (and they're there, for sure) and growing properly to maturity. We don't want to encourage their growth beyond normal levels in the root zones by mixing in wood, but having a lot of fungi at the soil level isn't going to bother the root zones.

So, mulch with wood chips and some sawdust if you like but do not dig this material into the soil.

One problem that is real with using sawdust as a mulch is that it compacts terribly easily. And this can block water penetration and restrict air circulation to the soil. If you have to use sawdust, then spread it thinly and do not allow it to build up to several inches in depth. But if you've already added sawdust or wood chips to the soil, simply feed extra nitrogen to the soil to provide enough nitrogen both to the bacteria and fungi needed to support your plants and degrade the cellulose. A weekly feeding with a nitrogen-rich plant food such as fish emulsion will solve this problem.

The Top 5 Reasons For a Permanent Mulch

1 It's a lot less work than digging or tilling every year. Toss a few bales of straw (available at many garden centres or farm stores) onto the top of the soil and you're done.

2 Moisture is evenly distributed throughout the soil and soil drying is reduced. Evenly distributed moisture conditions are perfect for increasing yields and reducing plant stress.

3 Composting is easy. Toss the compost on top of the mulch and let it settle in by itself. Let me repeat: No more digging!

4 Soil is cooler in the summer, protected from the sun's heat. This also increases yields (but it is slower to heat up in the spring).

5 The mulch degrades, feeding the soil and creating perfect soil microbiology for increased production and health of the vegetables. And a healthy vegetable that's high in nutrients is better for my family.

6 Bonus! Did I mention it's a lot easier?

If You Already Have a Garden

If you already have a garden bed you've been digging and using, simply mulch it with 7 to 10 cm of organic matter. If you have lots of leaves, use them. Otherwise, use whatever is locally available. Wood chips are my last choice because I like to have fast-degrading material on my vegetable gardens; I believe it feeds the soil faster if it degrades faster and this means better nutrition faster. Start adding as much compost and regular doses of compost tea as you can. You're now building your soil.

If you don't have a garden area yet, you can build soil slowly and easily or quickly and with more work.

The Quick-Work System

The quick-work system involves removing the grass, usually by digging it up and tossing it into a pile to compost.

Next, lay down 2 cm of peat moss and dig or roto-till it in. Yes, I did say that I no longer use a roto-tiller for maintenance, but for digging a bed the first time, a tiller is a valuable tool.

You've created some bare ground and taken the first step of adding organic matter to get that soil ready to produce vegetables.

The next step is to mulch everything heavily, then start adding compost and compost tea in order to bring the soil to life.

The quick-work system can be a lot of work depending on the size of your garden but you can have a working garden in a few hours. It will take some time for the compost and compost tea to build up the soil microorganism population, but you'll have a running start. Your garden soil will continue to improve from year to year.

The Slow-but-Easy System

The major difference of the slow-but-easy system is that instead of digging and removing the layer or sod or turf grass, you're going to put down a layer of cardboard or multiple layers of newspaper (overlapped so there are no spaces) to form an impenetrable barrier to prevent grass from growing through. You're going to shade out the turf, starve it of sunlight, and allow it to die in place.

I prefer to use cardboard to kill grass because it really does an outstanding job and is free at most food stores. I then pile on a few centimetres of peat moss, some mulch, and compost. I don't mix them in but just leave them sitting there.

To plant transplants, make a really small hole in the cardboard (a trowel driven in hard enough to penetrate the cardboard works, or you can use a garden knife tool, such as a hori-hori knife) and then carefully put the roots into the slot in the soil. You do get a bit of grass escaping through the hole but this is easily clipped off or just pulled up later in the summer. Or ignore it this summer; pull it in the fall or next spring.

The cardboard will become wet during the summer and will become pretty mushy. This isn't a problem because worms just adore the taste of corrugated cardboard and will work it into the soil faster than you can believe possible. In one step, you've managed to eliminate the grass without digging and start the process of adding organic matter to the soil.

The slow part comes in because it is going to take an extra year or two for the cardboard to disintegrate fully, for the compost and compost tea to populate your soil with microorganisms, and for your garden soil to become fully active. But it's a lot less digging.

And it doesn't matter which system you use because after you start, you're going to switch to mulching and composting regularly anyway.

What About Keeping the Garden Soil Bare?

You can do this, too. It's more work because you will have to keep the weeds out of the vegetable crop. Weeds compete very well with the more sedate vegetables and will outgrow them in most cases. But if you like bare ground, and I know gardeners who do, then weed away.

But continue to add organic matter, compost, and compost tea to improve the amount of microorganisms and organic matter levels. The health of your garden depends on these things.

How Much Water Do I Need?

This is a government answer: it depends. We know the proportion of water in most vegetables is in the high-80 percent to low-90 percent range. So you need to keep "adequate" water in the vegetable garden.

Most garden books will tell you that a garden requires 2 to 3 cm of water a week. But in my experience, it depends whether you are mulching or keeping the soil bare (bare ground requires more water). It depends whether you have the open, lovely, sandier soils of lower mainland BC, the heavy clays of some parts of eastern Ontario, or even the sandy rock of Digby, Nova Scotia. The more clay in the soil, the less water you "might" have to add. The "might" comes because it also depends on how much rain you get.

So here's my working advice, and like anything else, you'll modify this a bit as you gain experience. Pull back the mulch, drive a trowel about 5 to 6 cm into the soil, and lean the trowel a bit so you can see the soil 2 to 3 cm deep. Feel it—if it is damp, then don't water. If it is dry, then soak the garden with 3 to 5 cm of water or until it is damp 2 to 3 cm down into the soil.

With a bit of practice, you'll quickly learn how much to water by feeling the ground with your finger or by pulling a bit of soil back with your fingers. If your finger comes away damp from a few centimetres down, leave the soil be. If it comes away dry, then water.

Watch Out for Wilting

The amount of water you need with a mulched garden is less than it is with bare soil but you do have to check under that mulch regularly because you won't see the early "dry soil" look. Your first clue that plants need watering will be wilting leaves and this is never a good thing for a vegetable.

Overhead or Drip Watering?

Drip. There's no longer a choice involved, I'm afraid. The simple reason is that overhead sprinklers lose 50 percent of their water to evaporation. You can cut your water bill by 50 percent by using drip irrigation and this very quickly pays for any hoses you might have to purchase.

When to Water

In practice, water anytime you have the time to set it up. There's an old wives' tale that watering during the day will somehow burn plants because the water drops magnify the sun's rays. This is not true. You don't want to water during the heat of the day because you lose even more water to evaporation than you do at other times of the day.

Of course, with drip irrigation, it doesn't matter that much when you water, but if you have a choice (or you decide to do it by hand or by overhead), water in the early morning to allow the sun to dry off the leaf surfaces.

A Canadian Must-Know Garden Technique

The difference between most Canadian gardens and the rest of the world is that we get a real winter. It kills off our pests and forces us to rest and relax in front of an open fire. But what we really want is to extend our gardens for just that extra week or three when the early fall frosts are sweeping in. Here are a couple of tips to help you postpone Old Man Winter back a bit.

Cover your plants. You'll see blankets, sheets, cardboard boxes, and other kinds of coverings laid out over gardens on clear fall nights when frost is in the forecast. These work for a degree or two of frost. Clear plastic does not protect plants but instead allows the heat to escape.

Water your garden. The last thing at night and very early in the morning, water with a fine mist. In our nursery, we'd regularly get frosts after we put tender plants outside. So we'd simply turn on the sprinkler systems and cover the plants with a fine mist of water. The water freezes on the leaves (we referred to them at this stage as plant-sicles), but as the sun comes out and the water is still spraying, the ice would thaw and melt off the plant and all was right in the garden. The water would give off heat in the process of freezing and the plant would be fine through several degrees of frost. Simply understand you have to have the water going before the killing frost comes through and before the sun comes out. Again this technique is good protection for a degree or two of frost.

Container Vegetable and Herb Gardening

There are a few simple things you have to understand to ensure success when you're growing vegetables in containers.

➤ Vegetables are 90 percent (or more) water so if you allow your containers to dry out, you're going to reduce or eliminate your vegetable harvest. A perfect example is the tomato. We want to grow it everywhere and containers answer that need for balcony growers as well as those with no soil. But the minute the plant gets too dry, calcium stops moving up the plant to the fruit (the tomato) and it will develop blossom end rot (a black rotting on the bottom). It's not a disease; it's the result of poor watering practices and you only have to let the plant dry out once or twice when it doesn't want to and your entire crop is ruined.

So we need to really watch the watering and get it right. The easiest way to do this is to have huge containers. Forget tiny pots; anything smaller than a 30-cm flowerpot isn't going to make it. To give you an idea, I used to grow tomatoes commercially in green plastic garbage bags on the floor of my greenhouse. It took six full shovels of soil to give enough support to the plant and I had to water every day—sometimes twice a day—to keep those plants properly watered. They would dry out with six shovels of soil in a day. So *if* you can water every day or twice a day in the heat of the summer, you can grow vegetables in six shovels of soil. But if you want to skip a day (or a weekend), then you had better increase the amount of soil you're using. And that means larger pots.

➤ You need to feed your plants. When you water, any fertilizer that is in the soil is washed out the bottom of the pot or driven down away from the roots. If you want your plants to grow, you have to feed them. At my nursery, we fed every plant every time we watered so there would always be food there for them to eat. Bottom line: if you're not feeding every time or every second time you water, then your plants aren't getting enough food. A rule of thumb is to feed plant food at half-strength every second time you water.

➤ You need to keep the pots cool. I never use black plastic pots because the sun beats down on them and heats the soil. When the soil gets too hot, the plant stops growing (and dies if it gets way too hot). You see, we know that leaves start shutting down when the air temperatures reach 28°C. What isn't common knowledge is that when soil temperatures get into the 30° to 40°C range, plant performance is going to suffer. It is fairly easy for soil temperatures in a black plastic pot to reach above the 30°C mark on a hot summer's day. I use clay pots for this reason. They take more water than plastic pots but they are much cooler (because they don't absorb as much sunlight and evaporate/cool through water sweating out of the pot).

➤ Use the right kind of soil in your container. Fill the pot from top to bottom with a peat moss based artificial soil. Do not use real soil or any potting soil that contains real soil. The main reason behind adding the peat moss based soil from top to bottom is that putting shards or other material on the bottom of the pot to "increase drainage" is an old wives' tale. The second reason is that real soil compacts during the summer, turning into "concrete" and eliminating the air spaces that tiny feeder roots need to feed the plant.

➤ In answer to the question, "What can I grow in a container?" I propose the answer, "Anything you want." There is no reason you can't have

Prefer Fahrenheit? To convert Celsius to Fahrenheit, multiply by 9, divide by 5, and add 32.

your entire garden in containers on a back deck (away from deer, although they will wander up there if they're hungry), or on the cottage dock, or even right beside the tiny backyard patio in the midst of downtown. You can do it!

➤ There is no difference between growing in a container and growing in a small garden. The plant doesn't know the difference as long as you provide it with everything it needs, so you get to grow what you want! Grow all vegetables and herbs you like using the instructions in the specific sections later in this book.

The Container Basics Summary

➤ Water properly; soak so the water runs out the bottom every time you water.

➤ Use peat moss-based artificial soils from top to bottom in the pot.

➤ Feed properly every second time you water with half-strength fertilizer—a minimum of one weekly feeding.

➤ Give the plant enough soil in containers that don't absorb heat and look good.

➤ Grow what you want to eat.

Problems We See in Canada

We here in the frozen north have an interesting assortment of large animal pests that can get in the way of gardening. I've had readers ask about everything from black bear to elk controls (aren't you glad you garden in the city?) to raccoon and cat problems. This book isn't about controlling every animal problem, but I want to give you a few simple hints that seem to work for the majority of folks with the majority of animals.

Oh Dear, I See a Deer!

Deer are a major problem in all areas outside of heavily urbanized areas. There is nothing short of a dog or shotgun that will stop a hungry deer from eating any plant. Period. All the deer-resistant plants in the world won't stop a hungry deer. Some poisonous plants such as daffodils *might*, but even poisonous plants such as yew disappear when the deer are hungry.

The only solution that works close to 100 percent of the time is to build a properly constructed deer fence. A deer fence is the only thing that will stop a hungry deer (most of the time) but it has to be properly constructed of a heavy enough weight to stop a mature animal, and have exit gates to let deer out after that big animal has broken through.

There are several things to understand about controlling deer. The first is the psychology of controlling them. Deer like everything to be the same and shy away from things that are different. They move along predetermined pathways, and if you want to push them off those pathways you have to "encourage" them with alternate routes. This is the role of scented products (usually containing rotten egg odors). It's normally recommended that these products be changed regularly so deer don't become familiar with the fragrance. You want the deer to be skittish when they approach the property, not relaxed. I've seen many deer "fragrances" promoted in home remedies but the bottom line is to use them all and change them regularly; then, put up a deer fence.

You can also create psychological barriers that stop deer. For example, build raised beds with narrow pathways between them and fill the beds with plants so you can't see any ground. Then surround this with a short fence that will force a deer to jump inside. The deer has to jump into an area where it is unsure of its landing-space footing (narrow walkways and no empty ground). It will not jump this 1.2 m fence unless it is starving. Mind you, deer will enjoy everything *outside* of this fence. Also, a deer will not jump a solid fence it cannot see over unless it is being chased by dogs.

Finally, you can scare deer by using electronic garden gadgets. One product is a motion-detector–controlled water sprinkler that comes on when something trips the beam. It sprays out a few seconds of water and then resets itself. You can control a small area with each of these. An animal isn't hurt by the water-jet but it is startled enough to run away (at least a short distance until it figures out nothing is chasing it).

The Masked Deer

Raccoons are the urban equivalent to deer. These are serious marauders in the garden and can do an amazing amount of damage in a short time. For example, you can forget about growing corn unless you can control the raccoons, because they'll get there the day before you think a cob is ripe. Guaranteed!

Raccoons are not bothered overly much by traditional fences or by fragrance sprays. Using a motion-detector water sprinkler has been touted by some gardeners I know as being successful, as has employing a motion-activated, high-frequency noisemaker. The variability of both of these—only working when tripped—seems to have an effect, whereas leaving the sprinkler or noisemaker constantly on soon wears off.

You can install an electric fence in your garden and this works if properly constructed so a raccoon cannot get under, through, or over the top of a fence without making contact with the wires. These will not permanently harm any animal but they do deliver a shock that is an effective deterrent. I recommend wiping the wire with a rag covered in peanut butter to attract the animals to the wire (turn off the electrical source first). One shock is usually enough and raccoons (and other animals) will avoid the wire in the future.

Tips for Insect Control

There is absolutely no reason to have to resort to chemical insect controls in the modern garden. I ran an entire nursery organically, so managing insects in a small backyard garden is a walk in the park.

Never use any pest control product without reading the label. I know, I know, you get the same advice from everybody but all you want to do is wipe out whatever's eating your lettuce. Right, me too. But I've had folks write to ask why this fungicide wouldn't kill whatever was eating the lettuce. When I pointed out that it was an insect that was eating the lettuce, not a fungus, they had problems understanding that just putting "something" on the plant wouldn't fix it. Or worse, they put things that were intended for nonfood pests onto a food crop. More than once, I've had to tell readers not to use a systemic poison such as Cygon 2E on a food crop. Yes, it would kill the insect but then you'd be eating the leaves that were poisoned with something that could really kill you. Accidents such as this have happened in our food chain in the past and people have become very ill. So know what you want to control and read the label to make sure you're using the right product.

What to Look For

Damage that happens at night where you can't see any pest is often a slug. Look for slime trails on tender leaves. Tomatoes that appear to be eaten away in the middle from a small entrance hole is due to a slug.

Black "soot" on leaves or fruit is often from aphids (right). You should be able to see a small, pear-shaped pest on tender growing tips.

Odd, small holes here and there are often due to flea-beetles. These guys are really tough to see because they're tiny and jump very quickly at the first sign of leaf movements (like you trying to see them).

Big holes on cabbage and broccoli crops are usually from a green worm, which is the larvae of the cabbage butterfly.

Clouds of small white flying insects when you move leaves are whitefly.

Tomato plants that are disappearing before your eyes or overnight are being eaten by the tomato hornworm. If you're really quiet, you can hear the clicking of their eating. Squash them.

Squash leaves that disappear are normally due to squash bugs.

Good Organic Controls

There are a few organic controls that form the backbone for almost all the major pests.

The first is a jet of water from a hose. You'll be amazed at how quickly a strong stream of water knocks aphids and other crawling insects off a plant. No fuss, no muss, no residue, no mixing, no spraying, and no aphids! When they're knocked off a plant, aphids are helpless and become food for the larger beetles and other predators living at ground level.

Don't Take Chances

Read the label. Even organic products are not to be messed with.

Let me tell you a story. While running my greenhouse, I switched completely to organic controls and thought that soap sprays would solve problems we had in the propagation house. Although I had previously worn full spray suits with air packs to spray any kind of chemical, I assumed an "organic" spray wouldn't hurt me. This shows you that I did this way too many years ago and that I was a bit naive at that time.

I loaded up the soap into my fog sprayer, which is an electric sprayer that coats all surfaces with a fine mist and uses high air pressure to get under the leaves and coat the entire plant surface. I had a great insect kill and was quite pleased with myself.

Until ... I got an almost instant "cold" and had trouble breathing. I was wheezing away like a mad scientist. The soap that I had been breathing worked quite nicely to strip away the protective layers in my lungs as well as those of the insects. It took me about a week to recover my ability to breathe deeply. I have never sprayed an organic product since without full protection.

Just because something is organic doesn't mean it's harmless. It simply means it degrades into the environment quickly and safely without dangerous residues. It doesn't mean it won't hurt you or your family.

Read the label.

Insecticidal soap is a fast knockdown product for many of the soft-bodied insects you can see. Remember that you have to hit them with the soap to kill 'em. If you can't see them, you can't hit them and can't kill them. There is no residual power in the soap and once it is dry, it is pretty much done. Insecticidal soap has to be repeated regularly (read the label) and mixed properly so it won't burn the plants. It does tend to do interesting things to the colour of some blooms so check to make sure what it can be used on.

Rotenone is another fast knockdown product. This can be a lethal product for mammals as well as insects so wear protective clothing when using it. It only has a life span of 24 hours in sunlight and degrades naturally and quickly in the soil. You don't have to see the insects to kill them but it helps to understand what you're trying to control because it won't work on everything in the garden. Please read the label on this before you use it.

Diatomaceous earth is great stuff for crawling insects that you can't see. It is registered for a wide variety of pests and able to work for long periods of time. This is a very fine powder, the remnants of long-dead sea creatures. While the powder feels like talcum powder to us, to small insects it is composed of microscopically sharp shards. It would be like walking over broken glass to us. Insects are pierced by the shards and dehydrate. It's safe for animals, pets, and humans.

The jury is still out on **Neem**. You'll see it used in many countries for insect control. In Canada it is sold as a leaf-cleaning product and can't be advertised or recommended in any other way.

Iron phosphate is an organic product used in slug controls and is perfectly harmless to pets. It works like magic. Keep the beer to yourself from now on.

Bt (*Bacillus thuringiensis*) is a bacteria that paralyzes the stomach of caterpillar-type pests. They eat the bacteria, essentially get a stomachache, stop eating, and crawl away to die. They do not die immediately but they pretty much stop eating fairly quickly. This product, while registered in Canada for some insects, can be difficult to find at garden shops. The bacteria are alive so it has a relatively short life span. While it is available for commercial use, there are no sources for consumers at the time of the printing of this book. You will see it mentioned in American publications because it is available in the United States.

Those are the basics you'll use for the majority of your organic insect controls. I include the Neem so you'll understand the difference between the Canadian regulations and the advertising you're likely seeing coming out of the United States. Regulation may change in the future but at the time of printing this book, this was the situation.

INTENSIVE GARDENING

Growing More in Less

❦

Before we get into the meat of how you're going to grow healthy vegetables in small spaces, there are a few terms you should learn. Understanding the following terms and concepts will save you a great deal of trouble later when we're focusing on each one and again when we combine them. So rather than blather on, let's jump right into the important stuff.

The first term is "multiple cropping." This means that two or more vegetable crops are grown in the same space during one gardening season. You might put in a section of early spring peas and, in the same space, follow them with a crop of fall broccoli. The second term is "underplant," which means to tuck a second plant underneath or in the shadow of the first (and taller) plant.

"Intercropping" is another useful term. This means we're growing two or more different vegetables in the same garden section at the same time.

We could grow corn as a tall crop with an underplanting of pumpkins, for example. Farmers intercrop corn underplanted with clover or alfalfa.

Home gardeners don't garden on this scale, so we use the term "bed intercropping" where we divide our garden into smaller areas or individual "beds." Our beds are each treated like a farmer's field in that we'll plant several plants in each bed at the same time when we're bed intercropping.

In the home garden, we become very productive when we combine both multiple cropping with intercropping. Every square foot of garden space is constantly filled with a growing plant. When one plant is harvested, another is ready to take its place. Tall plants that take a full season to mature are underplanted with multiple crops of different vegetables.

This is a wonderful adventure in gardening and once you master these techniques, your garden size will shrink and your production will skyrocket. Welcome to the adventure!

First Steps

One of the interesting things that happens when we start putting plants together is that leaves and roots intermingle. There are a wide variety of effects created both in the root zone with chemical interactions and in the leaf zone with shade and overlap interactions. While we'll ignore the chemistry part of all this, in this practical section we'll outline the basics of what you're trying to achieve.

Long- and Short-Term Plants

Each vegetable and even variety within each vegetable has its own maturity date, and combining these different dates is covered in the graphics on pages 56 through 58. It is important for you to consider the maturity dates of the plants you want to grow so that you can always have something growing in each section of the garden.

While there is a difference between individual vegetables themselves (radish versus corn, for example), within each type of vegetable you can also find early and late varieties (such as early corn versus late corn) for almost every plant you'd consider growing.

This means not only can you plan around the difference between vegetables, you can plan on the difference within varieties of the same vegetable. You can plant early tomatoes in one bed and late tomatoes in another, for example.

Height and Growth Patterns Aboveground

It is important to know how your plants grow to interplant successfully. Some are vinelike (cucumbers, for example) that provide a living mulch. They'll grow very well if you give them a little support such as corn. Some, such as celery, are upright plants, and planting them next to floppy plants like beans will support the beans. Spreading plants with open-leaf patterns such as peppers grow very well next to squat, dense-leaved plants such as cabbage.

A Living Mulch

Remember that using this top-bottom planting combination system covers the ground so that no bare ground is left. You're creating a "living mulch" that shades the soil, thus preserving moisture and stopping weed germination. You can still mulch with organic matter but the top growth further reduces weed growth.

ABOVEGROUND VEGETABLE COMBINATIONS

Here are some plant combinations that grow nicely together with their aboveground growing patterns. While this isn't every possible combination, it will give you a good idea about combining your plants so the top growth is complementary.

bean – celery

bean – corn

bean – corn – squash, melon, or cucumber

bean – radish

bean – tomato (staked)

cabbage – chives

cabbage – cucumber

cabbage – pepper

cabbage – tomato

cole crop – carrot

corn – cabbage

corn – lettuce

corn – potato

corn – squash, melon, or cucumber

leek – carrot

leek – parsley

lettuce – carrot, onion

lettuce – onion

lettuce – radish

melon – radish

onion – carrot

onion – eggplant

onion – pepper

onion – radish

onion – spinach

peas on trellis – cole crop, turnip, lettuce, carrot, spinach, radish

sweet potato – pumpkin

Vegetable Gardening in the Shade

There are some important points you have to understand about reducing light levels in the vegetable garden. I add these here because some gardeners may be thinking of trying to grow vegetables in the shade and others will have noticed that growing corn and cucumbers together is going to create shady conditions for the cucumbers.

It is quite possible to garden under trees if you've got an "open-leaved" tree such as a fruit tree or a smaller or younger ornamental tree that doesn't produce much shade and allows sunlight to reach the ground. The same theory applies to the wide spacing of a large vegetable plant such as corn.

However, it is not possible to grow vegetables under dense shade trees such as evergreens or even mature dense-leaved maples.

Two Tricks to Keep In Mind

The trick is to use shade-tolerant plants under or beside trees that allow light to penetrate through to the ground. So think spinach and lettuce rather than big tomatoes.

Having said that, all varieties you plant have to be early-season varieties. You simply can't grow a late-season corn or tomato in the shade and expect a crop. You *might* get a crop if you use the earliest possible variety. Consider early varieties to be more shade tolerant in practice.

Each garden and the amount of shade in each hardiness zone are different every year (that's what makes this such an "interesting" challenge). The amount of shade varies from year to year based on weather, the surrounding plants, and location (locations such as the prairies get more hours of sunshine than the West Coast), and so forth.

The bottom line is you'll get to experiment and work with early varieties because they might grow for you where they won't grow for me. Try!

Shade-Tolerant Vegetables

Let me be clear: all vegetables prefer full sun but a few do "better" in a limited amount of shade than others. Better is a relative term meaning "not great but surviving to produce something."

Here are some of the most shade-tolerant vegetables and possible combinations of them for height and growth patterns. In this table, the second row of plants includes the more shade-tolerant plants. In other words, try to grow celery next to bush beans because the celery won't be too badly influenced by the shade. If you try to grow high light level cole crops next to bush beans, though, the cole crops would do poorly.

Again, use the earliest possible varieties you can find of each of these plants.

bean (bush) – celery	**cucumber (trellis) – celery**
bean (bush) – lettuce	**cucumber (trellis) – lettuce**
bean (bush) – spinach	**eggplant – celery**
cole crop – celery	**onion – carrot – lettuce**
cole crop – lettuce	**peas (trellis) – lettuce**
cole crop – spinach	**peas (trellis) – spinach**
corn – lettuce	**sunflower – cucumber**
	tomato (stake) – lettuce

Note that the words *trellis* and *stake* mean you *have* to grow that particular plant upright. It can't be allowed to sprawl on the ground.

NUTRITION

Feeding an intensive garden can be an interesting science experiment. There are entire textbooks devoted to feeding agricultural crops on full-sized farms. The vegetables perform the same; corn is still a greedy feeder of nitrogen no matter where you grow it, and peas will still leave more nitrogen in the ground than they consume. What differs in this case is not the needs of the plants but rather the economic consequence of failure or success.

There are a couple of ways you can deal with feeding your plants. You can learn the nutrition needs of every plant you want to grow, or you can "cheat" a little bit and simply use the following easy, home-gardener system. Naturally, I'd recommend the easy system.

Easy Home-Gardener System

➤ In the early spring, compost the entire garden. Work in as much compost as you have, ideally .9 kg per 900 sq cm (about .6 to 1 cm deep). If you don't have compost, use an organic matter such as peat moss. If you use peat moss or a similar matter, make sure you use compost tea to get the necessary microorganisms working. If you mulch rather than dig your garden, add an extra 2 to 3 cm of mulch to replace the lost mulch from the previous year and don't do any digging. (This is *my* preferred method.)

➤ Apply compost tea every 2 weeks, or at least monthly, for the growing cycle. This will ensure that adequate numbers of beneficial microorganisms are present in the soil.

➤ Feed each plant section weekly, or at least every 2 weeks, with a liquid fish emulsion fertilizer according to the heavy, light, soil-building notes (see below).

This simple system will give your soil adequate nutrition for the season without you having to figure out the particular demands of each crop.

A More Complex System: Planting by Nutritional Needs

If you want to set up a system for planting by plants, nutritional needs, here are a few guidelines that will help you.

Heavy feeders are those plants that demand a lot of nitrogen, including plants with large leaf surfaces such as lettuce, corn, and cabbage (and other cole crops), and vine crops such as squash. Feeding them a fish emulsion is best done weekly.

Light feeders are mostly root crops such as carrots and turnips. They tend to prefer heavier applications of potash. These plants will be fine with a feeding every 2 weeks.

Soil-building plants are the last group and these are plants that leave more nitrogen in the soil after they are finished growing. Beans, peas, and peanuts are three examples. These plants will appreciate a liquid feeding every two weeks.

Doug's Really Simple System

I know that organic gardening purists will cringe here, but a practical rule of thumb is that you can feed tomatoes, peppers, and eggplants with fish emulsion every week if you can remember. I want a heavy yield from these plants and I don't mind feeding with fish emulsion to get it. A thick organic mulch reduces the need for a weekly feeding. But the bottom line is, if in doubt, a little fish emulsion isn't going to hurt anything.

Doug's First Rule of Gardening

You only have to feed your plants if you want new leaves, flowers, or fruit.

Planting Rules

These guidelines give us several planting rules if you're not going to be applying the liquid fish emulsion. I don't recommend this but you might prefer not to feed your plants.

Never plant one heavy-feeding crop followed by a second heavy feeder in any garden bed. The second planting will find there is no nutrition left in the soil.

In a perfect world, you'd plant the soil-building crop first, followed by a heavy feeders crop, and then a light-feeding plant (for example beans, then lettuce, then beets).

Your Soil Savings Account

The single most important thing to be aware of in intensive planting is the health of the soil. You have to treat your soil like a bank savings account. It is necessary to put more into that soil than you take out if you want to keep it healthy. Negative garden soil nutritional balances lead to garden problems, and these will happen in intensive gardening systems far faster than they will in traditional systems.

Root Patterns and Spacing

If we were really trying to be serious about understanding the mechanics of large-scale planting, we would also categorize and plant our vegetables by the size of their root systems. In practical home-gardening terms, however, we already know the spacing of common vegetables and this is given in the table below.

As a matter of interest, the root size of a plant that is started indoors in a cell pack will be reduced when compared to a garden-started seed that is not transplanted. A started plant also uses less garden space. We can use this to our advantage in the intensive garden by starting our seeds in cell packs before we transplant them in the garden. This gives us quicker transplants, reduced root competition, and permits a more intensive use of garden space.

SPACING (IN CENTIMETRES)

Bean, bush	5	Leek	15
Bean, lima	5	Lettuce	70
Bean, pole	5	Muskmelon	60
Beet	5	Onion	5
Broccoli	60	Parsnip	10
Brussels sprouts	60	Peas	2.5
Cabbage	45	Pepper	60
Carrot	5	Potato	30
Cauliflower	60	Pumpkin	60
Celery	15	Radish	2.5
Chard, Swiss	30	Spinach	15
Corn	22	Squash	60
Cucumber	30	Tomato, unstaked	90
Eggplant	60	Tomato, staked	60
Endive	22	Turnip	10
Kale	60	Watermelon	60
Kohlrabi	10		

If you read a seed catalogue and the spacing requirements state "Plant 5 to 8 cm apart," then you're going to plant this vegetable 5 cm apart.

The health of our plants will be reduced when we crowd them into an area smaller than they need but it won't be reduced if we give them exactly what they require but no more. This is a fancy way of saying we don't want to get more vegetables by crowding our plants. Instead, we want to get more vegetables by growing them in exactly the space they need and by multiple cropping as well as intercropping (see page 44 for definitions).

The Critical Spacing Rule

Here's what you need to know about spacing: if you're going to be intercropping, plant a crop like radish together with lettuce. To decide how far apart to plant any two plants, take the sum of their individual spacing needs and divide by two. In this case, the radish requires 5 cm and the lettuce requires 30 cm. So, 5 plus 30 equals 35; 35 divided by 2 equals 17.5 cm.

Plant the radish and lettuce 17.5 cm apart.

Temperature Preferences

Here's where we get to the meat of the matter. While it may sound complicated at first, these tables will give you some clear data about which vegetables will work together. This is one of the key variables in intensive planting.

The reality is that we face two distinct kinds of problems with our vegetables when it comes to temperature preferences. The first is that some crops require specific temperatures to grow properly.

For example, peas and spinach will only grow well in cool soils and cool temperatures. These crops simply don't grow well in hot temperatures. You'll want to plant these in the spring and fall to avoid the heat of the summer. Some plants such as potatoes will grow both in cool and warm soil, so you can plant early or late, harvesting early or late depending on the variety and how large you want the tuber to be.

Other plants such as tomatoes and peppers will only grow in warm temperatures, so you'll have to plant them after the ground has warmed up.

The second of these temperature-related problems is where you're gardening and how long your growing season is. If you live in a zone 3, then your short season is going to mean that a plant such as a tomato is going to occupy one growing area for the entire growing season and your interplanting will be growing shade-tolerant plants around its base. You simply don't have the time to ripen a crop of radish or spinach before those tomatoes have to go into the ground. However, if you live in a zone 7, you'll very well be able to harvest a spinach or pea crop before the tomatoes are planted. I can just do this in my zone 5 garden.

Cool-Loving Plants

All of these dates are approximate but are set for a zone 5 garden. For every zone that's warmer, you can adjust by planting roughly a week sooner. All sowing and cell pack growing is done indoors; transplanting refers to outdoor transplanting. If the transplant section is blank, it simply means the sowing is done directly outdoors and is not transplanted.

CROP	SOW	TRANSPLANT	HARVEST
Beet	mid-March	mid-April	early May
Beet – crop 2	mid-April outdoors	early May thin	late June
Broccoli	early March	mid-April	mid-June
Brussels sprouts	early March	mid-April	mid-June, early July
Cabbage	early March	mid-April	mid- to late July
Carrot	early March	mid-April	late May
Carrot – crop 2	mid-April outdoors	thin as appropriate	late June
Cauliflower	mid-March	mid-April	early July
Celery	early March	early May	early July
Endive	early March	late April	mid- to late June
Kale	early March	early April	early May
Kale – crop 2	early April	early May	late May
Leek	early March	mid-April	late July
Lettuce	late March	late April	late May
Onion	early March	early April	late June
Onion – crop 2	early April	early May	mid-July
Parsley	late February	mid-April	end May
Parsnip	early March	mid-April	mid-July
Pea	mid-March outdoors	late May	
Pea – crop 2	late April outdoors	late June	
Potato	mid-April outdoors		early July
Radish	early April outdoors	early May	
Radish – crop 2	early May outdoors	early June	
Rutabaga	early March	early April	late May
Spinach	late March	late April	mid-May
Swiss chard	late March	late April	late May

Mid-Season Plants

These are the plants that thrive on summer's heat and do not grow well in cool soils or cool air temperatures. These are planted after the cool-temperature crops have had their day in the sun.

CROP	SOW	TRANSPLANT	HARVEST
Bean	mid-April	end May	mid-July
Carrot	end May		early August
Corn	mid-May	mid-June	mid- to end August
Cucumber	mid-May	mid-June	end July
Eggplant	mid-April	end May	mid-August
Melon	mid-April	end May	end July
Pepper	mid-April	end May	mid-August
Potato	end May		mid-September
Pumpkin	early June	mid-October	
Squash, summer (continual growing)			
	mid-April		end June
	end May		mid-August
	end June		mid-September
Squash, winter	mid-April	end May	end August
Squash, winter	end May		mid-September
Sweet potato	mid-April	end May, early June	early September
Tomato	end March	end May	mid-August
Watermelon	end April	end May	mid-August

Late-Season Plants

Then we have the plants that grow well in the shortening days and cool air temperatures but still warm soil of the late summer and early fall.

CROP	SOW	TRANSPLANT	HARVEST
Beet	mid-August	mid-September	end Sept., early Oct.
Broccoli	end June	early August	late September
Brussels sprouts	mid-June	end July	October
Cabbage	mid-June	end July	October
Carrot	mid-July		late September
Cauliflower	mid July	end July	October
Celery	early July	mid-September	October
Chicory	mid-July	mid-August	October
Kale	end July	mid-September	October
Kohlrabi	mid-August	mid-September	October
Lettuce	end August	end September	October
Onion	end June	begin August	October
Parsnip	end June		October
Pea	mid-July		October
Radish	mid-August on weekly		end September on
Spinach	end August	mid-September	October
Swiss chard	mid-August	mid-September	October
Turnip	early August	early September	October

Putting It All Together

We want to ensure there's not a single square meter of garden space left unplanted so we're going to match our plants for height, sited next to plants with complementary leaf coverage, in a sequence of planting and transplanting from early April right through to harvesting in October.

As one plant is harvested, another transplant is ready to go directly into its space.

Theory vs. Reality

The theory is really nice in all of these intensive planting schemes but the hard, cold reality is that it takes a lot of work and a lot of planning (not to mention constant attention to the small details) for this kind of gardening to really be successful. You may decide to implement a few of these things in your first attempt using only the plants you really like to eat. Multiple crops of salad "stuff" like lettuce and spinach are the easiest first step. After you master those, go onwards from there.

Another useful point to keep in mind is that the timing of each of these crops will vary from garden area to area. The times here are scheduled for a zone 5 garden and if you live in a warmer or colder area, you'll be able to adjust your timing accordingly. And just to really make you frustrated (join the gardening club here), every season is different. We'll have a cold, wet spring one year and a short, hot one the next. All of these planning steps have to be flexible and there is no one-size-fits-all every season.

Having said all that, it is fairly easy to begin if you take the following steps.

Steps for Success

1 Pick the cool-season vegetables that you want to grow. Decide how many times during the season you can grow them (check the early, mid-, and late season crop tables). Do not bother growing plants you'll never eat or that you eat infrequently.

2 Decide how best to combine them in the garden. Figure out which plants should go next to other plants (refer to the aboveground growing pattern section).

3 Decide which plants can tolerate some shade and put them in combination, if you can. (Check out the shade-tolerant section.) Try to put the shade-tolerant plants under or next to the sun-demanding plants.

The best advice I can give you is to always combine a long- and a short-term crop in the same bed if you possibly can. That way, you'll be growing the long-season crop and harvesting the short-season crop.

Crop Rotation

One thing that farmers do that home gardeners should copy is to rotate their crops. They try to avoid growing the same plant in the same space for more than two or three years in a row. By switching plants, the diseases and pests that like any particular crop are reduced because there is nothing for them to eat.

Home gardeners need to do the same thing. Never grow the same plant in the same space two years in a row. By rotating your vegetables, you'll reduce insect problems, disease problems, and you'll get a better yield from the plant when you do return it to that original bed.

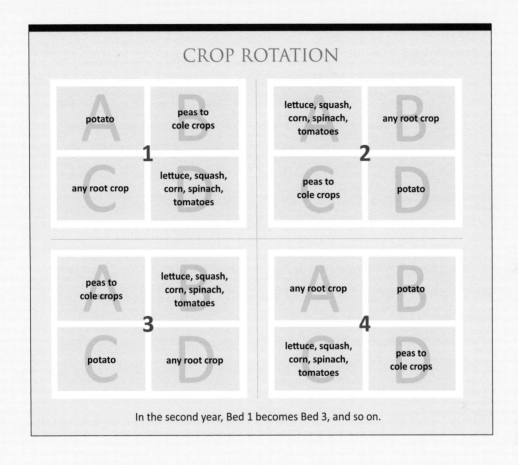

CROP ROTATION

1
- A: potato
- B: peas to cole crops
- C: any root crop
- D: lettuce, squash, corn, spinach, tomatoes

2
- A: lettuce, squash, corn, spinach, tomatoes
- B: any root crop
- C: peas to cole crops
- D: potato

3
- A: peas to cole crops
- B: lettuce, squash, corn, spinach, tomatoes
- C: potato
- D: any root crop

4
- A: any root crop
- B: potato
- C: lettuce, squash, corn, spinach, tomatoes
- D: peas to cole crops

In the second year, Bed 1 becomes Bed 3, and so on.

This is an example of a small bed crop rotation scheme. It is not intended to be an example of succession planting.

There are four groupings of plants that we plant together:

➤ potatoes pretty much by themselves
➤ peas and cole crops such as broccoli and cabbage
➤ any root crop, such as carrot or beets (but not potatoes)
➤ lettuce, spinach, tomatoes, and squash family members

There are four main beds, labeled 1 through 4. Each of the beds is broken down into four smaller growing sections (a) through (d). Each of the groups listed in the preceding paragraph gets its own bed. If you don't grow potatoes, you can use the potato bed as a second bed of one of the other groups or divide your garden area into three rather than four sections.

An easy and effective crop rotation system is to grow this pattern in year one. In year two, move Bed 1 to the area occupied by Bed 3. Keep the sections the same in Bed 1 when it moves. In other words, Bed 1a moves to Bed 3a; Bed 1b moves to Bed 3b; Bed 1c moves to Bed 3c; and Bed 1d moves to Bed 3d.

Move Bed 3 to occupy Bed 4. Bed 4 goes to Bed 2 and Bed 2 goes to Bed 1 in a counterclockwise rotation. Or, you can do it clockwise if you prefer. The important thing is that you make a plan and stick to it from year to year. What exactly goes into the beds is up to you but this plan works well if you don't want to go to the bother of figuring out your own.

Draw this up for your own garden for the plants you like to eat.

A Simple Intensive Gardening System

Using the diagrams of crop rotation, let us design a very simple system for spring, summer, and fall cropping. These are designed for my own garden, so you'll want to modify them for your own.

In any bed that had empty space, I'd transplant a seedling flower or herb from another bed to fill it or let it grow. I'd grow some of my perennial seedlings by using the extra vegetable garden space.

You'll also note that Bed 1 is double dug and heavily composted in the spring rotation and Bed 4 is planted with green manure in the summer. (Green manure is a plant such as buckwheat or oats that is turned under while it's still green to increase the soil's organic matter.) In this way, each bed is given a soil-building treatment every second year, along with the normal spring composting. But this is simply what I'd do; it is optional if you apply enough compost in the spring.

Spring

You see the spring garden is half double dug. I can produce enough salad stuff in half a garden to feed myself and half my friends. I simply don't require the entire garden space, so I spend some time building soil in the spring. Now, if I had four kids at home, this layout would be different. Make it work for you.

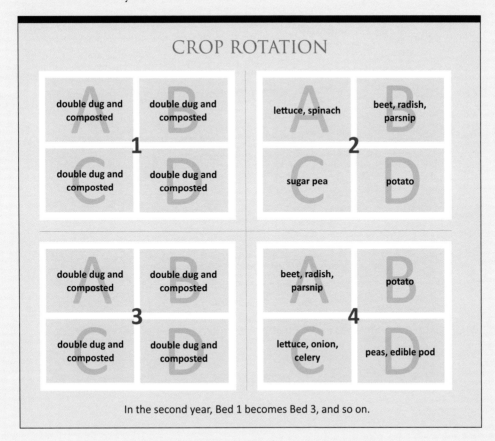

CROP ROTATION

1

A	B
double dug and composted	double dug and composted
C	D
double dug and composted	double dug and composted

2

A	B
lettuce, spinach	beet, radish, parsnip
C	D
sugar pea	potato

3

A	B
double dug and composted	double dug and composted
C	D
double dug and composted	double dug and composted

4

A	B
beet, radish, parsnip	potato
C	D
lettuce, onion, celery	peas, edible pod

In the second year, Bed 1 becomes Bed 3, and so on.

The summer garden is where I start to lay in the plants for real production. Each bed is filled to capacity and the occasional dead plant is replaced immediately with a flower or herb transplant.

Again, I use a soil-building buckwheat planting, but I could reduce the size or number of beds if I wanted to reduce my workload.

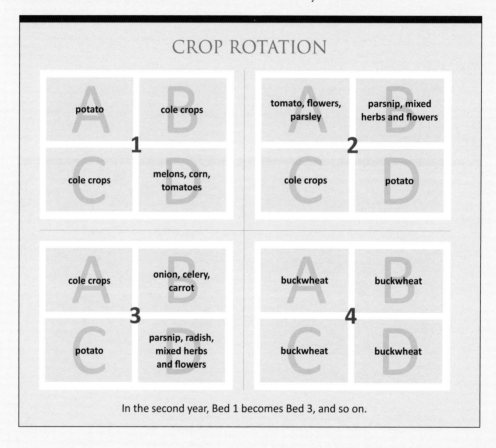

CROP ROTATION

1
- A: potato
- B: cole crops
- C: cole crops
- D: melons, corn, tomatoes

2
- A: tomato, flowers, parsley
- B: parsnip, mixed herbs and flowers
- C: cole crops
- D: potato

3
- A: cole crops
- B: onion, celery, carrot
- C: potato
- D: parsnip, radish, mixed herbs and flowers

4
- A: buckwheat
- B: buckwheat
- C: buckwheat
- D: buckwheat

In the second year, Bed 1 becomes Bed 3, and so on.

Start with What You Want

My primary system really starts with a blank sheet of graph paper for all three seasons, and I fill in the main crops I really want to grow first. Sugar peas go into spring; tomatoes go into their space in summer. Corn goes into its space. My few herbs and trial flowers go into their spots and times. Then I fill up the remaining space with other stuff. Start with what you really want to grow and insert it for the season; then fill in the other spaces.

Fall

Because of my cold garden, many of the main season summer crops are hanging in and repeated below until fall. I'll continue harvest from these plants until frost takes the tender ones out. Then the frost-hardy fall crops will continue.

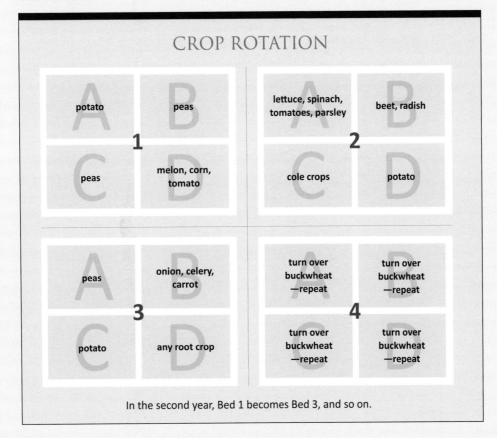

CROP ROTATION

1

A	B
potato	peas
C	D
peas	melon, corn, tomato

2

A	B
lettuce, spinach, tomatoes, parsley	beet, radish
C	D
cole crops	potato

3

A	B
peas	onion, celery, carrot
C	D
potato	any root crop

4

A	B
turn over buckwheat —repeat	turn over buckwheat —repeat
C	D
turn over buckwheat —repeat	turn over buckwheat —repeat

In the second year, Bed 1 becomes Bed 3, and so on.

Thinning Isn't Just About Hair

One of the things I'll refer to in this section is "thinning"; this is where you remove unwanted seedlings. The interesting thing here is that these plants are not wasted; you can eat some of them, particularly the leafy vegetables such as lettuce, mustard greens, and spinach, while you transplant others such as broccoli and cabbages.

You don't have to thin all at once. Normally, with a crop such as lettuce, you thin when the new leaves start to touch each other. Remove every second plant so those plants left in the row don't touch anymore, and eat the thinned lettuce. Then, when the lettuce leaves start to touch again because they've grown up, thin again by removing every second plant or the third, or whatever combination removes plants and allows the remaining plants to continue to mature.

In this way, you space out your plants, use the smaller plants, and choose the strongest ones to remain in your garden. That's the other criteria to use when thinning the rows. Pick out the weaker plants, the smaller ones that aren't growing so well. By leaving the strongest, you'll encourage that plant to grow to maturity and give you a larger crop.

While most instructions say thin "every second or every third plant," in reality you get to make some decisions about which plants to take and which are bigger (removing the weaker ones). Sometimes, you'll wind up taking a larger plant simply because it's in the wrong space—that's okay. The objective is to wind up with lovely, well-spaced rows of plants of uniform size, but frankly, this usually happens only in magazine pictures. My straggly rows usually wind up looking like I've been harvesting them all summer. But my kitchen salads are always full of fresh pickings.

So don't worry about creating picture perfect rows; simply remove the weakest and try to space the remaining plants equally in the row as they grow.

1 Set up a graph of your garden and draw it into beds on paper, if not in fact.

2 Make three copies of the graph, one for spring, summer, and fall.

3 Put the vegetables, herbs, and flowers you really want to grow into their unique spaces for the season; for example, draw in your tomatoes into the summer and fall sections.

4 Fill in the rest with the secondary crops based on when they grow best. Try to combine plants using my suggestions for height, spacing, leaf shape, and so forth.

5 Don't worry if it doesn't work out properly. It never does. Get as close as you can and understand that most gardeners fill in the garden too much on paper. We gardeners are such optimists.

6 Relax and have fun!

Random Thoughts on Intensive Gardening

While I've said it previously, it is important to consider the fertility and health of your soil in intensive gardening. You'll "use up" that soil much faster when you practice multiple cropping. This is why I recommend using a lot of organic matter and weekly feedings of fish emulsion.

The size of a bed can be as large or small as you want to make it. Each bed can be as small as a single square metre in smaller gardens or as large as a farmer's field if you have the inclination (and a strong back).

My own bed sizes have varied over the years depending on how many kids were at home, what we were growing, and how much work we needed to do. My current bed size is approximately 1.25 m by 1 m wide.

The major difference is that I'll have extra beds for perennials and cut flowers that will be season-long beds. But with the exception of the perennial bed, which will move every 3 to 4 years, all specialty flowerbeds will be rotated through this kind of cycle.

"Plant" your garden on paper. There is no way you can hope to design intercropping and multiple cropping in your head, especially if you're just beginning. Draw it as accurately as possible on graph paper or on a computer; a spreadsheet package works quite nicely for designing beds.

Set up a planting timetable. You'll note that you'll be moving transplants into place almost all summer. In order to transplant into the garden in August, you'll want to have started the seed in the house or in your seed-starting area in June. Set up a seeding schedule on a calendar that you refer to regularly. This is why I suggest you start small with a single crop or two of lettuce or spinach (or any plant you love to eat) to get you going with this system.

Some beds are easy to plant. For example, in the fall, Bed 1b only contains peas. But Bed 2a contains lettuce, spinach, tomatoes, and likely some leftover parsley. The lettuce and spinach transplants will have to be "fitted" around the existing plants to achieve the proper spacing.

This is easier to do in practice than it is in theory. In theory, you're trying to figure everything out ahead of time and the first time can be overwhelming. In practice, you look at the garden and say, "Heck, the tomatoes and parsley are still growing strong; let's just fit a few spinach and lettuce transplants in here and there to fill up this bed."

The most important rule in gardening is to enjoy yourself and not worry if your plans don't work out quite the way you intended. They never do because Mother Nature always has the last word and she's an opinionated old soul.

There are few things nicer in the garden than being able to walk out and munch on a freshly picked vegetable. You know it is fresh. You know it is healthy. But above all else, you know it tastes really, really good.

And that's the beauty of growing your own food. Every small garden has space for some fresh tomatoes, some basil, and some other odds and sods that produce a salad or two along with those famous toasted tomato sandwiches (the ones that drip down your chin).

I wish you as much success and enjoyment in your garden as is possible to wish for another.

VEGETABLES

I could write for a long time about growing vegetables but the main thing you really need to know is that growing your own vegetables is worth the effort. There is absolutely <u>nothing</u> like the taste of a sun-ripened tomato picked from your own garden and sliced onto a heavily buttered toast for a tomato sandwich, all accomplished within a few minutes. You won't believe the sweetness of corn that goes from garden to pot to plate in three minutes. Getting kids (of all sizes) to eat their veggies is easy if you let them grow and pick sweet, edible-podded peas; there'll be a lineup in the garden to pick them. Just don't expect any peas to get to the table . . .

I've put exactly what you need to know to grow great vegetables in this chapter. This information has been distilled from literally years of answering vegetable gardening questions in my own nursery and Internet writing. Happy growing and set a place at the table for me!

ASPARAGUS

Asparagus is one of the greatest plants for an early spring garden and you either love them or hate them. I happen to love the garden varieties but I still collect the wild spears in early spring.

When to Plant

There are two ways to start an asparagus bed—the fast, expensive way or the slow, inexpensive way. Fast and expensive is to purchase the roots you'll need. The slow and inexpensive way is to grow from seed.

While it is possible to start seed indoors in January, the easier way is to sow directly into the garden in mid-April. Soak seed for 48 hours before sowing by laying them on a damp paper towel. Asparagus seed is a very slow germinator; it takes about 30 days.

Where to Plant

Plant in full sunshine in your best soils. Do *not* plant in clay soil as any tendency toward waterlogging will rot the roots.

How to Plant

Dig a trench approximately 10 cm deep. Sow the seed 2 to 3 cm deep in the bottom of the trench and space the seed several centimetres apart.

After seed germinates, thin to 12 cm apart. Over the summer, gradually fill in the trench with soil while you are cultivating. Mulch over the winter to protect the young roots. The following April, before they start to emerge, dig up all the roots.

The fast folks will simply purchase asparagus roots while the slow gardeners will have spent a year growing their roots.

Dig a trench in the garden approximately 20 to 30 cm deep and 30 cm wide. Set the most vigorous roots 25 to 30 cm apart. Space the rows 1.2 m apart.

Cover the roots with 5 to 8 cm of soil but do not fill in the trench. Over the course of the summer, gradually fill in the trench as described previously. By the time fall arrives, it will be filled in without a lot of extra work. You want the spears to grow while you slowly backfill the trench; doing it all at once will delay their growth.

Care & Maintenance

Do not harvest spears the first year! You can take a single harvest the second year, the first week that spears appear. After that, allow all spears to grow foliage. By the third year, you should be able to harvest for 6 weeks. Allow all spears after this to mature.

Control weeds by using an organic mulch. Mulch also evens out the soil temperature, provides protection to the asparagus roots, and increases organic matter.

Additional Information

If you find your spears are thin, you are not feeding enough; spears should be thumb-thick. Thicker spears are the tastiest and these will be produced early in the season.

Leave the foliage alone until it turns yellow-golden brown in the fall; then you can cut it down and compost it.

Control asparagus beetle by handpicking, rotenone, or diatomaceous earth.

BEET

Pickled beets might be one of my favourite types of pickles and there are not many things in the vegetable patch that are nicer than harvesting smaller beet roots and taking them right to the kitchen for processing.

When to Plant

If you really like beets, sow every two weeks from the earliest time you can sow seeds in your garden. That would be as soon as you can work your garden soil without it staying "clumpy," usually about a month after snow melts. Sow regularly until the middle of July.

If you want extra-early crops, you can sow them in a cold frame and transplant to the garden, but this is a lot of work and will only give you 1 to 2 weeks advantage over soil-sown plants. While this may have a commercial value, in the home garden it is a lot of work for very little return.

Beet seed does not rot as quickly as more tender seed and it starts to grow along with spinach, lettuce, and peas (other early sown vegetables). It will not grow if the soil is colder than 4° to 5°C, but will sit until the soil warms up.

If you want to store or pickle beets in the fall, count back ten weeks from your harvest date and plant the crop then.

Where to Plant

Plant in full sun in a loose, sandier soil. Heavier (clay) soils are tough to grow in.

How to Plant

Sow seed approximately 1 cm deep.

Twenty-eight grams will be enough to plant 30 m of row. At 5-to-7 cm spacing, this translates to 400 plants in a 30 m row. If you are growing tiny plants for pickling, reduce this spacing interval to 2 cm apart. Lengthen or shorten the row depending on the number of vegetables you're going to eat.

Care & Maintenance

On average, harvest when the tops are 15 cm tall. This will give you the tenderest roots. If you leave the crop to get really big, there is an increased risk of a beet getting "woody" and not as sweet to eat.

If there are heavy rains after a long dry, hot spell, you might find white rings in the beets. They are still edible although not cosmetically perfect.

Additional Information

It is far cheaper to purchase seeds than to purchase starter plants from a greenhouse. This plant is very easy to grow. The seeds can be saved from year to year if you keep the seed dry and cool. Do not freeze the seed.

You can store beet roots in the refrigerator for several months without any loss of quality.

BROCCOLI

Broccoli is an extremely valuable vegetable when it comes to providing a full range of vitamins and minerals (not to mention fibre) to our diets. This is a plant for healthy eating and it is no wonder that mothers have been saying for years, "Eat your broccoli!"

When to Plant

Early crops should be sown indoors approximately 6 to 8 weeks before you want to plant them outdoors. The seeds are easily germinated so do not crowd them in the seedling tray. Space them at least 1.5 cm from any other seed. When a seedling has four true leaves (leaves that develop after the first two seedling leaves), transplant it into a larger container for growing on. Full sunlight, regular feeding at half strength, and a temperature of 16°C will produce a nice short, thick plant for putting into your garden.

Late crops can be sown directly into the garden from early May until the first week of June in zones 3 to 5 gardens and as late as July in warmer areas. Sow the seed—4 to 5 seeds per 30 cm. Remember that this seed germinates quite easily. Then thin out or transplant the resulting seedlings so they are 45 cm apart. Generally, broccoli will mature approximately 100 days from the day you sow it.

Where to Plant

Plant in full sun in good garden soil.

How to Plant

The transplants should be put into the garden 45 cm apart and the rows 75 to 80 cm apart. Try to put the plant at the same depth in the soil as it was in the pot. Planting a trifle deeper is better than shallower.

Care & Maintenance

Harvest broccoli when the large central heads are still tightly budded. While you can eat them when the buds begin to swell and open, they are much nicer harvested when they're tight.

Do *not* pull up the plant but simply cut off the top head. The side shoots will develop and you'll get a ton of these from each plant. Harvest side shoots regularly, before they start to stretch or the buds open on them. These smaller heads are easy to pick and are great used fresh in salads and stir-fries.

Additional Information

The major pest of broccoli is the green caterpillar of the cabbage moth. Dust with rotenone or handpick to control this pest. Dropping the harvested heads in salty water will also help to identify the "surprises" you miss. Chewed-up leaves is the primary sign that you have an infestation.

If you are concerned with cutworms (small worms that eat the stems below the soil line), you can wrap the stem with a band of waxed paper or heavy paper to stop the worm from getting to the stem. A very tiny bit of lime or wood ash scattered around the plant will deter slugs. Alternately, you can use an organic slug bait around your transplants.

BRUSSELS SPROUTS

Brussels sprouts are one of those vegetables that you either hate or love. There's very little room in the middle on this one. If you love 'em, you'll be really pleased to know how easy they are to grow.

When to Plant

For the most part, treat this plant exactly as you would a late cabbage crop. (see page 72). It is so easy to sow and grow outdoors that starter plants should be outlawed.

Where to Plant

Plant in full sun in moderately fertile soil. As with other members of the cabbage family, Brussels sprouts like an open soil with good drainage and do very well in soils high on organic matter. An even supply of water will produce a significant number of sprouts for harvest.

How to Plant

After the last frost around the end of May, sow seed very thinly at 1 seed per cm approximately .6 cm deep. Do not bury too deeply. About a month later, when the plants have four true leaves, thin out the row so that plants are spaced 45 to 60 cm apart.

Excess seedlings can be carefully dug up and transplanted to give you a longer row. They move quite easily at this stage.

Care & Maintenance

You'll get much higher yields if you ensure your soil is well fed, preferably with good compost before the season starts and an application of fish emulsion during the season.

With a well-grown plant, you can figure on 75 small sprouts per plant. Harvest Brussels sprouts when the sprouts reach 2 to 3 cm across. Start from the bottom and work your way up the plant. You will find that this plant is very frost tolerant and that sprouts that have been *lightly* frosted seem sweeter than those harvested before frost. You should be able to harvest 4 to 5 times to get all the sprouts over a 5-to-6 week window.

Additional Information

If severe frosts threaten your area, you can pull an entire plant out of the ground (roots and all) and hang it upside down in a frost-free area. Continue to harvest the sprouts until they are gone. Compost the remaining plant.

Pests are the same as for any member of the cabbage family and you'll have to watch for both aphids and cabbage worms. Generally, we don't see much of any other pest.

BUSH BEAN

You know, I was never a fan of bush beans until I discovered how good they tasted in stir-fries. Then I became a big fan and have eaten them regularly over the past few years. I just hate it when people overcook this vegetable; if it doesn't still have a snap, it's overcooked.

When to Plant

The biggest problem with beans is that gardeners try to plant them too early. The ground temperature should be around 15°C before you put a bean seed into the ground. If you're using untreated beans, this translates into the first week of June in a zone 4 garden. If you succumb and purchase fungicide-treated beans, you can plant a week or two earlier. The warmer the soil, the better the germination rate.

If you want some good beans, plan on sowing every two weeks until the end of June or middle of July in warmer areas. This should give you enough fresh beans to keep you harvesting and enjoying the plants until frost knocks them down.

Hint: Never plant a white-seeded bean too early or it will tend to die off on you. You can cheat a little with darker seeds. Apparently, the white seeds have a thinner seed coat and absorb water too quickly so that the early seeds crack and die instead of growing.

Where to Plant

Plant in full sun in a good soil. Soils high in organic matter produce better crops.

How to Plant

Seeds should be planted approximately 5 to 8 cm apart in the row and the rows should be 60 cm apart. Do not plant them too deeply—no more than 1.5 to 2 cm. Deeper is simply burying, not sowing.

Care & Maintenance

Compost tilled into the garden before planting will get the beans going as soon as they germinate.

As with most vegetables, do not work in the garden when the plants are wet. Bean rust, anthracnose, and blight are easily spread to nearby plants by moisture on the plants.

Additional Information

A single plant will give enough for one meal for two people, so plan according to the number of people you expect to feed and the number of meals you want.

Shipping beans have extra fibre to stop the bean from cracking and breaking during shipping. Don't freeze them.

Fresh market beans are tender but they get lumpy quickly as the bean inside matures. They're ugly and they contain a medium amount of fibre. But they taste good. Harvest regularly to avoid the lumpy look.

Processing and gourmet beans have the least amount of fibre and are extremely tender. These are the beans for freezing or canning. They are influenced by bad or cold weather so never plant them early.

CABBAGE

Cabbages are very easy plants to grow and belong in the garden of every serious vegetable gardener.

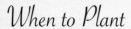

When to Plant

If you want very early crops, sow the seed eight weeks before you intend to plant them. The early cabbages need indoor starting if they are to be harvested early. Sow the seed in flats about .5 cm deep; planting too deep kills them. The easiest way to do this is to lay the seed on a firmed bed of soil and then barely cover them.

Otherwise, sow seed outdoors in late May or early June about .5 cm deep.

Keep the soil temperature fairly high—22°C is minimum—and you'll see seedlings in 4 to 5 days. Once they emerge, drop the temperature immediately to 12° to 14°C or you'll produce long, leggy seedlings, for sure.

About 4 to 5 weeks after seeding, they should have four true leaves (not the tiny seedling leaves) and be ready to transplant into a small flowerpot or a transplanting pack. You want them to develop their own roots. Approximately ten days before you want to plant them start leaving them outside in the daytime to harden them off. You want a tough plant, not a tender seedling that will croak under wind and sunlight. Bring them in at night to protect against frost and cold winds.

If you harden them off properly, a very early crop of cabbage can be put into the ground about the same time as you can dig and prepare the ground (usually late April or early May in my garden). Hardened-off plants can stand quite a bit of frost.

Where to Plant

You can grow cabbage in just about any soil although a well-drained, fertile soil high in organic matter is best. Even moisture levels are important to stop splitting. You'll often see cabbages splitting later in the season when they are given water after a dryish spell; they grow so fast they split. They require full sunlight or they'll get long and leggy.

How to Plant

Cabbages are generally planted 45 cm apart in rows.

You can direct sow cabbage although direct sowing is generally reserved for later crops. Sow at 1 seed per 3 cm and thin to 1 plant per every 45 cm as they grow. Harvest when the leaves start touching; you'll get small baby cabbages early on and much larger harvests when they mature.

Care & Maintenance

The old timers used to drive a shovel down beside a plant to cut off half its roots when it got big enough to harvest. This prevented the plant from taking up too much water and splitting. Enough roots remained to keep the plant alive and healthy.

Additional Information

Problems are generally cutworms, aphids, and cabbage worms.

CARROT

Carrots are one of those vegetables that gardeners often fail to grow successfully. There are just a few simple things to understand and once you deal with those, carrots are no more difficult to grow than any other vegetable.

So what's the secret? The real secret to growing great carrots is to double-dig the garden soil. A deep, well-composted soil will grow terrific carrots. Raised garden beds will also grow great carrots if you take the time to make super soil in those beds.

When to Plant

Sow every week from the last frost date in your area until midsummer to avoid any bad weather that would surely knock out some of your crop.

Where to Plant

Sow seed in full sun in your best soils. The more organic matter in the soil, the better.

How to Plant

Sow carrot seed very thinly in a row. Some gardeners mix radish seed with the carrot seed so they'll be able to tell where the row is.

Soil temperatures should be at least 15° to 16°C before sowing carrot seed. Seed should be sown so there are 3 to 4 seeds per every 2 to 3 cm of row. Rows should be 40 to 45 cm apart.

Sow by laying the seed on the surface and then covering it very lightly with .6 cm of soil. Tamp the row down gently to make sure the seed is in contact with the ground. If you bury this seed deeply, you'll never see carrots. Water gently with a fine nozzle on the hose to soak the ground; keep the soil damp until germination.

Care & Maintenance

If you overfeed them, you'll likely get roots with *a lot* of small feeder roots. (Remember the feeding rules for root crops!) It'll look like the carrot has grown a head of hair. Cracked carrots are caused by too much water at harvest time or allowing the carrot to get too old before harvesting.

Most of the problems are going to be with the soil. If you compact the soil around the neck of a carrot then your carrot is likely going to "fork," or grow extra roots, or otherwise be stunted or mis-shapen. Walking in the row too close to carrots will quickly compact the soil. Carrots do not like having to drive themselves down into the soil; think of them as lazy vegetables. If the soil is right, they'll grow long and straight. If not, you'll get terrible looking crops.

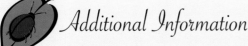 Additional Information

Sudden weather changes, late frosts, or cold seasons will result in really rough looking carrots. If you let them dry out or give them way too much water, you'll find they'll look ugly.

If you have a clayish soil, do not let the soil crust over or the carrot seedlings won't be able to penetrate the crust.

If you see "green shoulders" on some carrots, it is a good idea to very gently hoe up some soil around the shoulders to prevent or reduce this.

CAULIFLOWER

Cauliflower are easy plants to start and grow. Where home gardeners get into problems is by trying to obtain the white heads (or at least white like the ones you see in stores). It is all about attention to detail and variety selection.

When to Plant

Sow the seed around the beginning of March for a May transplanting to the outdoors (8 weeks before you want to put it into the garden).

Plant seeds approximately .6 cm deep. They germinate around 21°C. It should only take 7 days for seeds to germinate and some will be up in 5 days. Once the seeds have germinated, grow them a bit cooler, 15° to 16°C, but no colder because if the seedlings get too cold, about 10°C, they'll wind up bolting (going to flower) in the field instead of setting a head.

Harden off the transplants and set outside after danger of frost has passed. While the plants themselves can take frost, the cool nights will cause them to bolt later on.

Where to Plant

Like all the cole crops (such as broccoli and cabbage), this plant loves full sun in a good soil that is high in organic matter.

How to Plant

Transplants should be put 45 cm apart in the row and rows should be .75 m apart.

You can direct sow the seed outside after the middle of May right up to the middle of June and still get a good fall crop. The seeds should go down

.6 cm deep and about 10 cm apart.

When it comes to thinning in about five weeks, you'll want to choose the thinnest and straightest plants. Throw away any seedling that looks like it is swelling (and trying to set a head already). Transplant the extra to other parts of the garden. Thin to 1 plant every 45 centimetres.

Care & Maintenance

Here's the part that folks don't seem to get right. When the developing head (called a curd) is about the size of a coffee cup, take the big outer leaves and tie them up over top of the curd. Use rubber bands to keep the leaves firmly over the curd so that no light can get into the middle of the plant. (This is to keep the curd white.)

Blanching will only take a few days, 10 at most, and the head can be harvested. The warmer the weather, the quicker the curd will turn white (3 to 4 days if it is really hot). The head continues to grow while it is being blanched and you end up with a decent-sized head that is a nice white colour.

If you let the curd get too big, it simply won't turn back to clear white or stay yellow (it's more like an ugly cream). It is still edible; it's just ugly.

Blanching is why, by the way, you need to control cabbage worms as they eat holes in the darned leaves, which lets light through. If the leaves are too small or too holey you can place a paper bag over the curd (not our first choice, but it works).

Additional Information

Control the major pest of cauliflower, which is the cabbage butterfly, using organic methods.

CELERIAC

Treat celeriac much like celery in the northern parts, sowing indoors and growing on exactly the same way. The cautions about low temperatures apply equally to both vegetables.

When to Plant

For very early crops, sow the seed indoors the end of February. Plant seed .5 cm apart, or so. I say "or so" because I simply lay the seed down on a pot or flat, barely covering it with more soil to keep the seed moist; you can almost see the seed. Keep the soil damp. It doesn't need darkness to germinate and you'll see seedlings within 15 to 21 days depending on soil temperatures.

Transplant outdoors after frost or sow directly into the soil when the soil is quite warm (from the end of May to early June).

Where to Plant

Plant in full sun in a soil that is high in organic matter and where stress on the plant (such as watering too much or too little) is eliminated.

How to Plant

You can start celeriac in individual peat pots (2 seeds to a pot and thin to the strongest) if you only want a few, but the easiest method is to sow the seed directly outdoors.

Direct sow at 3 seeds every 1.5 to 2 cm and thin out the plants to 15 cm apart when the plants are approximately 10 to 15 cm tall. Sow .6 cm deep.

Celeriac is a slow germinator (15 to 21 days, depending on weather) so it is a great idea to mix radish seed with the celeriac as a "marker" seed. You can harvest the radish and thin out the celeriac at the same time.

If you plant more than one row of this plant (although I have absolutely no idea who would eat that much!), then plant rows the standard .75 m apart for good air circulation.

Care & Maintenance

Harvest the rounded, small turniplike roots when they are 5 cm in diameter. They taste kind of nutlike and do not require any blanching to make them whitish. If you let them get larger, they get woody.

You can store celeriac if you cut the tops off and cover them with dry sand at temperatures of 2.5° to 5°C.

Don't store them in the same container or area where there are very strong odors such as from cabbages or onions; they'll quickly pick up that smell.

Additional Information

See celery for more details; they are the same kind of grower.

CELERY

I always like growing my own celery because I think it has flavour. The stuff you buy in the store is essentially water wrapped around some fibre. Crunchy stuff in a salad and that's about the extent of it. The celery you grow yourself has leaves with flavour for soups and stir-fries and the stalk itself is worth using (although it might be a little tougher than "store-bought").

When to Plant

If you want some very early crops, sow the seed indoors the end of February.

Plant seed very shallowly, .5 cm or so (lay the seed down on the pot or flat and cover so you just lose sight of the seed).

The seed will germinate in 15 days (plus or minus 5 to 7 days) if you keep the seed flat around 22°C. Commercial growers raise the daytime temperature to 23° to 24°C and lower the night temperature to 18°C for increased germination.

Do not allow the seeds to dry out (but don't swamp them, either) as a steady moisture level will assist in germination. When the plants germinate, grow them at 18°C for good, stocky plants. If you let them get too cool in this growing-on stage, 12° to 13°C, they will tend to bolt in the field and go to seed rather than give you a leafy stalk.

Where to Plant

Plant in full sun in a moderately fertile soil. The trick is to give them constant sunshine and moisture levels.

How to Plant

The seedlings should take 3 months to get 10 cm tall and can be transplanted outdoors after all danger of frost is finished. If you screw up and your seedlings are taller than this, simply whack them back to 10 cm tall with scissors.

This will check their growth but you'll get a better plant in the long run than if you put them outdoors and they're leggy. (They flop around and don't do well when leggy.)

As with any crop, harden off the transplants before planting. Hardening off will give you a better chance of success. At this stage, be very careful because if your plants get too cold, they will bolt (flower) rather than grow leaves.

Plant the celery transplants 15 cm apart in the row. Rows should be 75 cm apart.

Care & Maintenance

This is a very shallow-rooted vegetable so you have to make sure it doesn't suffer from drought (it will get tough), root damage from cultivating too close (it will get tough), and lack of food (it will get tough).

Feed every few weeks with a liquid fish emulsion to keep the plants growing well and avoid—what else—toughness.

Additional Information

I hope the message got through that celery wants warmth and pampering or it will get tough. If your previous attempts have produced something less than ideal results, just think "pamper this plant" and you'll do fine.

CORN

I don't care what you grow in your garden—nothing can beat a freshly picked cob of corn. Period. End of discussion.

When to Plant

Plant corn about two weeks before your area's last frost date. The warmer the soil, the better the seed will germinate. Cold soils will rot the seed, so early plantings will be sparse and sporadic germinators. Better to plant a little later than too early.

Where to Plant

The nice thing about corn is you can grow it in almost any kind of soil—from sand to clay—but always in full, hot sun.

How to Plant

Plant your seed about 1.2 cm deep—no more—approximately 15 cm apart for the early varieties and 20 to 22 cm apart for the bigger, later varieties.

A row should be 3 to 4 m long at a minimum and you'll need 4 rows so the corn can cross-pollinate. Rows should be .6 to .8 m apart. If you plant your corn in a single row, expect to get missing kernels or misshapen cobs (or both). The minimum you should consider planting will be about 28 gms of seed for the 4 rows of 3 to 4 m length each; 28 gms of seed will sow approximately 15 m of row.

Never leave any seed showing in the row. If you do, a bird or beast will find it. And then they figure out that where there's one kernel, there has to be more.

Care & Maintenance

Corn is a greedy feeder so extra helpings of compost and a once-a-month dose of liquid fish emulsion will help to grow sturdy, tall plants.

Additional Information

Although corn is a tough plant, weather conditions influence the size and shape of the cobs. Cold nights in late June will make the cobs quite short but, like all things in the garden, there's little you can do. Just understand that some years you'll get long cobs and some years you'll get the short guys. Later plantings will be more uniform.

Many commercial seeds are treated with a fungicide. Seed that has been treated is more resistant to rot but it is not considered organic. Untreated seed should only be planted when the ground is at 18°C, and that's around the beginning of June in an average year in zone 5.

Sometimes, small cobs are produced near the bottom of the plant. Do not harvest or remove them; that will apparently slow down the growth rate of the main crop of corn.

Stop bird damage by putting small paper bags over the cobs as they mature.

Control borers or ear worms by applying mineral or horticultural oil to the silks. I have no idea how to stop porcupine or raccoon damage, other than by electric fencing or trapping the beasts. I can now tell them apart: porcupines lean against the stalks and knock them down while raccoons can break the stalks or simply reach up to harvest the cobs.

CUCUMBER

Cucumbers are so easy—and cheap!—to grow from seed that it is almost criminal to purchase starter packs from a garden shop. Started plants will be set back, particularly if they were rootbound in the pack, when they're transplanted and will not give any advantage in harvesting earlier.

When to Plant

Plant after the ground has warmed up nicely, late May to early June in most parts of the country. Later plantings will catch up to early plantings.

There is a technique for starting seeds in peat pots (the kind you can bury) two weeks before you want to put them outdoors. Plant one seed per pot, let them germinate, and plant the entire pot without damaging the roots in transplanting. Plant the peat pot so that its top is *at* the soil line; don't bury the stem of the cucumber.

Where to Plant

Plant in full sun in a soil that has even moisture supply. Remember that cucumbers are mostly water and will suffer in droughts or rot in too much water.

How to Plant

Plant seed approximately 1.25 cm deep in the garden. In the garden, cucumber seed is normally planted in hills; hoe the garden soil into a "hill" or mound approximately 7 to 9 cm above normal ground level and

.6 m across. Plant 6 to 8 seeds in a hill. Space hills 1.25 to 1.8 m apart. Thin to 4 plants per hill when the cucumbers grow 4 true leaves.

If you are planting in a row, put 2 seeds in each hole and place the holes .6 m apart. The rows should be 1.5 to 1.8 m apart.

Care & Maintenance

Consider thinning hills to only four plants by snipping off excess seedlings when they are approximately 5 cm tall. In row culture, snip off 1 of the 2 seedlings in the row when it is 5 cm tall. Normally, you allow the seedlings with the most vigorous growth to survive.

Water regularly but do try to keep the vines dry. Drip irrigation is perfect for cucumbers.

Pick cucumbers regularly to keep the vine producing. If you stop picking, it will stop producing.

Additional Information

Earlier plantings may be covered with Reemay™ frost cloth or given some other form of protection.

If you are gardening in a small space, you can train the cucumbers to climb up netting or snow fencing supported on posts. Train the central leader, the fastest growing and original shoot, straight up the fence until it gets to the top. Then prune it off level to the top of the fence. This 1.3-m vine will then develop multiple side shoots, which will bear profuse amounts of fruit.

EGGPLANT

Eggplants are one of those "sometimes" types of crops in many Canadian gardens. I confess, while it is easy to start eggplants, there are a few things to consider in growing them.

When to Plant

Purchase started plants or, to get the early variety you want, start them yourself. Sow seeds in mid-March for a late May outdoor transplant date.

Do not consider direct sowing as this will not work in most parts of the country, even in good years; this is a heat-loving plant.

Where to Plant

Plant in full sun in your warmest section of the garden, in your best and most fertile soil, out of wind and other cooling influences.

How to Plant

Plant the seed approximately .6 cm deep—no deeper. Keep the soil a minimum of 22°C—26°C is even better. Water with lukewarm water. The seed will germinate irregularly; you'll see several seedlings a day over a period of a week.

Once the seedlings have reached the 2- to 4-leaf stage, they can be transplanted into individual pots and grown at air temperatures in the low 20°s C.

While some seedlings do not mind being transplanted at a slightly lower depth (tomatoes thrive on it) always transplant eggplants at the same depth as they were in the seedling flat.

Keep the plants growing strongly with high light levels, regularly give them warm water, protect from cold drafts, feed regularly, and give them adequate spacing. Any check in growth will cause lower yields. You really want to avoid letting these plants go below 18°C when you're growing them.

Care & Maintenance

Transplant outdoors after all danger of frost, after the ground has warmed up and nighttime temperatures will not fall below 10°C. Cool nights mean that the flowers will fall off and you won't get a harvest.

Use a good amount of compost in the soil before planting (they love even moisture levels and even food levels). If the flowers set fruit, then feed with some fish emulsion or other organic-based food to give them a boost.

Additional Information

You might want to pinch off or carefully support any fruit that are touching the ground as they will tend to rot. But if that's all the fruit you have,—don't pinch expecting more. Expect to get 4 or 5 fruit per plant and you can harvest them as soon as they get to one-third their mature size.

Eggplants are bothered by the same pests as tomatoes and potatoes. To avoid wilt problems, do not grow them on the same ground where those plants have been grown in the previous two years. Control pests such as aphids and potato bugs with organic methods.

ENDIVE/ESCAROLE

Home gardeners are going to find that this is a perfect fall crop. Endive simply doesn't do very well when it's spring started because it runs into summer heat. I prefer the extended cool temperatures of fall. You *can* start it in the spring; just understand you won't likely get as good a crop as with a later sowing and fall harvest.

When to Plant

If you want to grow a spring crop, sow outdoors in mid-April in zone 5. Adjust your timing up or down for every zone different than zone 5. Sow outdoors in mid-June in all but the coldest zones for a fall crop.

Where to Plant

Plant in good soil in full sun.

How to Plant

Sow .6 cm deep at 1 seed every .2 cm.

Seeds want soil temperatures of 7° to 10°C to germinate. They will not germinate if the soil temperatures are higher.

The seed is also light-sensitive. This means you do not cover the seed. Firm the soil where you want to plant. Lay seed down on soil and firm seed into the seedbed so it is in contact with the soil.

Care & Maintenance

Thin maturing plants to 25 cm apart.

The big outer leaves must be tied up (loosely) around the heart of the plant to blanch the center (or hearts).

This plant, with its shallow roots, will benefit from a feeding of fish emulsion in midsummer.

Additional Information

One of the things you have to take care with is rotting of the heart. Every second or third day, untie the wrapper leaves and check the heart for rotting. This uncovering allows excess moisture to escape and will go a long way toward preventing rot.

Endive tastes and acts like lettuce. The main differences are that it is more work with all that tying and untying and it is really heat tolerant; lettuce hates high growing temperatures.

This plant will stand upright in the garden right through the first light frosts and will take deeper frosts if mulched heavily. It will not survive a serious killing frost, however.

The good news is that some folks believe endive actually tastes better if it's been lightly frosted.

GOURD

There are two ways to grow gourds in the home garden. You can sow indoors to get an early start on the season or sow directly into the garden's soil once the soil temperatures have warmed up. Luckily for us, you can grow just about any kind of gourd, from tiny ornamentals to the birdhouse forms right through to the most weirdly shaped fruit you can imagine.

When to Plant

If you're sowing indoors, seeding by the middle of April gives you lots of time to get a gourd vine up and growing before planting outdoors.

If you're going to plant gourds outdoors directly into the soil, wait until the soil has fully warmed up, usually the second week of June in zone 4.

Where to Plant

Plant in full sun in warm soils. A well-drained and fertile soil is best. Heavy clay soils are not the best for gourds.

How to Plant

Plant at 3 seeds to an 11-cm pot and thin to one strong seedling once 4 true leaves (real plant leaves, not small seed leaves) have grown.

Start at a soil temperature of 21°C. Transplant, being careful not to disturb the roots, in the middle of June once the soil and night temperatures have warmed up. Space plants approximately 1 m apart.

Outdoors, sow the seeds 1 to 2 cm deep in hills or rows. Hills should be approximately 1 m across and 3 plants per hill, or space the plants 60 cm apart.

Care & Maintenance

When the stem starts to shrivel and brown, the gourd is ripe.

After harvesting, wash the gourd with a strong disinfectant to remove any dirt; gourds seem to rot quickly if they're left dirty.

Dry thoroughly for 3 to 4 weeks. When the gourds are dry, wax with a good floor wax and they'll keep for a long time. Note that shellac and varnish tend to change the gourd color. Let the kids spray paint if they want; it will not harm the fruit.

Additional Information

Try growing gourds up a trellis if your space is limited; they climb quite well and the fruit stays cleaner. The smaller fruit can be easily left alone to ripen but the larger ones (over 1 kg) should be supported as they grow so they don't bend or pull the stem and vine down. I'd recommend some old pantyhose tied to the trellis under and around the fruit to remove the weight from the stem.

HORSERADISH

Horseradish has been cultivated in gardens for a very long time. In fact, we have records that say the Egyptians used this plant before 1500 B.C. and it is one of the "bitter" herbs used in Passover traditions. Believe it or not, it was also used as an aphrodisiac; mind you, the Romans used just about everything as an aphrodisiac.

When to Plant

The roots of horseradish are what we grow to eat. They are planted in the spring as soon as you can work the ground. Plant roots 15 cm deep and 30 cm apart (it has a vigorous top growth).

Where to Plant

Plant in full sun to light shade. You can grow horseradish in almost any soil except very heavy clay.

I always found the horseradish roots to be pest and disease free and they grew from year to year with no work on my part. This plant is easy to grow in full, hot sunshine and once you have it, you won't lose it (although it doesn't spread unless you leave roots in the ground).

How to Plant

Plant horseradish where you expect to grow it for a few years. Every bit of root left in the ground becomes a new plant the following year. Leave a 15-cm-long chunk of root wherever you want a plant for the subsequent year when you harvest in late summer or early fall. I always love those recommendations that call for thinning horseradish roots by pulling up the "extras." I think I could thin mine with a 100-horsepower backhoe (about the same size as the one I used to dig the farm pond). This is a tough plant.

Care & Maintenance

Very little care is necessary. Harvest anytime after midsummer when you want some roots, or in the fall when you're cleaning up your garden.

Additional Information

Now, the heat value of the root is not evident until you grate or grind up the root. It is at this point that the volatile oils (called isothiocyanates) are released.

For mild horseradish, add vinegar immediately after grinding. For hotter sauce, wait overnight to add the vinegar. The longer you wait to add the vinegar, the hotter the sauce will be because vinegar stabilizes the production of the oils.

When you grind horseradish, do so in a well-ventilated room. This stuff is as potent as very hot peppers. I like using a blender to whip it up and then I leave it for a bit to get the "heat" I want. I wash the roots and remove the skin and any dirt before I grind as I'm a little fussy that way.

One recipe calls for 2 to 3 tablespoons of vinegar (1 tablespoon equals 15 ml) and a half-teaspoon (1 teaspoon equals 5 ml) of salt for every cup (1 cup equals 240 ml) of horseradish. A friend told me she uses lemon juice instead of the vinegar. Store in a refrigerator until you use it.

KALE

Kale is a member of the cabbage family but it's one of the so-called "loose-leafed" forms. It is perhaps one of the simplest vegetables to grow because cold weather doesn't bother it at all; in fact, cold weather makes it taste a whole bunch better. I don't bother with it during the heat of the summer but plan on eating it in the fall and late fall when everything else has died off.

When to Plant

Kale is best sown as a fall crop but it can be a spring crop by over-wintering it.

For fall crops, sow the seed in mid-June to the end of July directly in the garden.

If you have the good fortune to live in a climate where zero degrees is as low as it gets over the winter, you can mulch the kale and it will provide a great crop of spring greens for early salads before the early lettuce and spinach can be harvested. After the other greens are available, pull up the kale and resow later in the season for best growth and taste.

Where to Plant

Kale likes what other members of the cabbage family like: full sun, well-drained soil high in organic matter (add lots of compost), and fertility.

How to Plant

Sow kale seeds at 1 to 1.25 cm deep. Thin the plants to 30 cm apart with rows .75m apart. These small, thinned-out plants make excellent salads, by the way. It also helps to gently tamp down the soil over the seeds to "firm up" the soil so the soil and even moisture are in contact with the seed.

Care & Maintenance

You can harvest this plant one of two ways. In October after your first frost, you can cut down the entire plant and use it like you would spinach in salads or cooking. Or, you can harvest the inner leaves as they mature because they taste better than those big outer leaves. You can harvest the inner leaves right up until snow buries the plant. And just before snow comes, harvest the rest of the plant for the kitchen. It will keep in the refrigerator for a surprisingly long time.

Additional Information

Kale has also been bred to produce multicoloured leaves and is used as a hardy ornamental plant for fall colour. These forms are as edible as any other kind of kale.

Try to rotate crops so that no other member of the cabbage family is in the same garden spot for two years before you plant kale there. Keep kale well watered during the heat of the summer and you're in business.

KOHLRABI

Kohlrabi is one of the weird-looking vegetables in the garden but it can be grown rather easily if you follow a few simple guidelines.

When to Plant

You can start it indoors if you want a really early crop. Sow the first two weeks in March for a late April transplanting date outdoors. It will require a soil temperature of 21°C to germinate and then a much cooler 12.5° to 15.5°C growing-on temperature to prevent leggy growth.

With direct sowing, you can put it into the ground from early May until July and it is often recommended that you sow several crops several weeks apart to get tender roots on an ongoing basis.

Where to Plant

Plant in full sun in soil where water and fertility is well managed. That means no droughts and no flooding.

How to Plant

Indoors, sow the seed approximately .6 cm deep. Each seed should be transplanted into its own small pot after it has three true leaves and grown on until transplanting outdoors.

Outdoors, sow seeds at 1 every 2 to 3 cm. When they start to grow and get a little crowded, thin to 1 plant every 10 cm. Harvest the small roots (eat them!) and thin out as the plants get larger to 1 plant every 30 cm apart.

Care & Maintenance

Kohlrabi is a very greedy feeder and will really benefit from adding a ton of compost to the soil where you intend to grow it. Feed every two weeks with a compost tea or fish emulsion to keep it growing strong.

It also likes to grow steadily (like cauliflower) so avoid dry spells by getting out the hose.

Actually, you'll find if you do stress it, the roots will become woody and you won't want to eat them. So water and feed this plant for decent edible crops, or don't bother.

Additional Information

Harvest all roots when they are smaller than a baseball as the larger roots can get woody. And do harvest the roots before fall nights get too frosty; this plant doesn't like cold temperatures in the fall.

You might see some flea beetles on kohlrabi but they are easily controlled by techniques listed on the organic controls on pages 38 to 42.

LEEK

You can grow leeks either as an early spring crop similar to onions or as a late-season crop by direct sowing into the garden. Either way, they are tasty!

When to Plant

For the early crop, sow seed in pots or flats as shallowly as possible approximately 6 to 8 weeks before you want to transplant them outdoors. Leeks shrug off cold soils and late frosts if well grown, and planting in late April is common in zone 5.

If you want a late crop, dig a 15-cm-deep furrow and plant the seed directly into the furrow the first week of September.

Where to Plant

Plant in full sun. Leeks like rich, fertile soil so adding compost is necessary if you want a great crop. They also do not like being water starved.

How to Plant

Sow seed .6 cm deep, cover, and gently firm the soil. Keep the soil temperature at 18° to 21°C for indoor plantings; you should see a germination rate of 75 percent or so within 2 to 3 weeks. Leek seed does not germinate as quickly or as completely as onions. If you have the ability to cool the seeds down at night, they'll germinate a little bit better. Daytime temperatures around 21°C and night temperatures around 15.5°C will give optimum germination.

As soon as you can get into the garden (late April), transplant them outside. Dig a 15-cm-deep furrow and plant the leeks at the bottom of this furrow. Over the course of the growing season, the trench gradually fills in when you cultivate nearby. This will also blanch the leek. Seedlings should be planted approximately 10 to 15 cm apart. Thin to 15 cm when the crop really gets growing.

Care & Maintenance

There are two schools of thought about the tops when you start your own plants. The time-honoured method says to trim the tops off, cutting the leek halfway back, when it gets 10 to 15 cm tall. The thinking is that this bulks up the root and makes transplanting better. The second school says not to cut back the tops as this retards the performance in the garden (which has been verified by at least one research study). I never cut them back after I read the article. Whichever method you select, after they germinate, grow them at 10°C to keep them short and blocky. Higher temperatures will cause them to get too tall and perform badly in the garden.

Leeks are usually dug in October before a really hard frost softens them. They are often used fresh but they will keep for a long time stored in frost-free conditions.

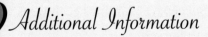

Additional Information

Feed every week with a balanced fertilizer to keep leeks growing strongly.

If you keep the frost away from them and bank them with straw, they'll start growing again the following April, which will make them very early to harvest and eat.

LETTUCE

Lettuce is an interesting crop and I find it usually does best if you sow them directly in the garden. If you start early, be careful when transplanting or you'll lose the starter plant. With their small roots and large leaves, lettuces can lose a lot of moisture very quickly on a hot day (particularly if you wreck their roots when transplanting).

When to Plant

Sow seed outdoors .6 cm deep as soon as you can get into the garden (late April) and then every week thereafter.

If you want to start them indoors, plant your seed in individual cell packs or peat pots approximately 6 weeks before you want to put them into the garden.

Where to Plant

Plant in full sun in soils high in organic matter.

How to Plant

Sow approximately 1 seed per centimeter of row and thin them out as they grow so that the mature lettuce will have 20 to 30 cm of space. Note the thinnings are perfect for eating! Successive plantings each week will give you a regular amount of lettuce to harvest.

For indoor sowing, remember that you do not want to disturb the roots of transplants if you start them early, so space the seedlings well and thin to one per cell or pot. Keep the seed warm for the first few days, but once they germinate, the lettuce plants should be grown no cooler than 15°C.

Care & Maintenance

You should be able to harvest one mature outer leaf per week from each plant; this should tell you how many plants to grow.

Once the heat of the summer hits, lettuce can go bitter, particularly if you water-stress it. So, keep the water flowing and plan on a fall sowing for fall harvests when the weather turns cool again.

Additional Information

Leaf lettuce is far easier to grow than head lettuce and I'd recommend it as a first effort in lettuce. You'll always get useable leaf lettuce leaves, while with the head lettuce, sometimes things happen to wreck the crop (like slugs or the head splits, for example). Note that those perfect heads you see in the supermarket are often hydroponically or greenhouse grown. Leaf lettuce growing follows the same rules but the harvest is done by taking a leaf or two from the outside of each plant. Do not pull up the plant but allow it to keep producing new, fresh leaves for harvest.

MELON

There are fewer things nicer in my summer kitchen than sun-ripened melons filled with vanilla ice cream. I don't care whether we're talking muskmelon or cantaloupe—I'm a big fan.

When to Plant

For early and reliable crops in zone 5 and colder, sow inside around the middle of April to the beginning of May. Sow 2 to 3 seeds to a 10-cm pot and thin to the strongest seed when the vines get 10 to 12 cm tall. You *must* have warm soil to germinate melons (21°C) and you'll find the seed will germinate within 10 days. Cool soil will rot the seed.

Where to Plant

Plant in full sun in your best well-drained and fertile soil.

How to Plant

After all danger of frost has disappeared, harden off the seedlings. If you're a melon fan, try this technique. (Note this technique is slightly different than the one described on page 20. The difference is you're going to want to keep the soil warming up until midsummer when you remove the plastic.) Take a black garbage bag (green works well, too) and cut it open so that it becomes one large sheet of plastic. Lay this down in the garden and bury the edges so they don't flap or flop around. Do this two weeks before you want to transplant.

Around the middle of June when you want to transplant, make a slit in the plastic bag, take the plant out of the pot (carefully, so you don't wreck

the roots), and plant in the warmed soil. Leave the plastic in place until midsummer. Then it should be removed, as it will heat up the soil too much for good crops. If you have a heat-retaining fabric, lay it over the plants and tuck in the edges so it doesn't flap about. Remove it when the plants start to produce flowers to allow bees to pollinate. And watch for birds that get trapped under the row-cover; they can make a mess of things (and it will happen).

You can sow the seed outdoors in mid-June but cool seasons will slow germination and eventual fruit production drastically unless you live in a gardening area much warmer than my zone 5 garden.

Care & Maintenance

Vine roots are very shallow so any cultivating has to be done carefully. And never move the vines as they really resent being moved about and will respond by wilting and sometimes simply dying.

Do not allow this plant to be water stressed during the growth or fruiting season. Stressed plants either don't produce fruit or the fruit is bitter.

Additional Information

You'll find that gentle pressure on the fruit at the base of the stem will disengage the ripe fruit; this is the easiest way to tell if a melon is ready to harvest. Do not disturb the vines if you can avoid it while testing for ripeness.

MUSTARD GREENS

If you need a quick-growing spring green that's easy to grow and tastes like spicy spinach, this is your plant. It is also an excellent source of vitamin A. This plant is normally considered a "southern" plant but we northerners can grow it in the spring and fall. Having said all that, mustard greens can also be a noxious weed if you let them flower and set seed in your garden. This is a two-edged sword of a plant—good to eat but a danger and a weed if it's not controlled.

When to Plant

Plant as soon as you can walk on or work the soil without it leaving huge clumps. This is the earliest vegetable to plant in the garden and you can't kill the seed if you only plant it .1 cm deep—barely cover the seed, if at all.

Sow a few seeds every week for the first 4 to 6 weeks of spring. Stop after that because mustard greens will bolt and go to seed very quickly when the weather warms up.

Sow again in August or September when the nights start cooling down.

Where to Plant

Average soil, of little or no fertility, is necessary, as is a sun or light shade location. If you have a sense you can grow this spicy green almost anywhere, you're right.

How to Plant

Plant .1 cm deep and 2 to 3 cm apart. When the leaves start to touch, thin the smaller plants (eat them!) until the mature plants are approximately 20 cm apart.

Care & Maintenance

There's little care needed for mustard greens. It's fast growing and seed will germinate in 3 to 7 days. Generally, you're going to thin out the seedlings around the 10-day mark and be ready to harvest mature plants in 50 days. In a good growing year, you can get early harvests about a month after planting; simply use the outer bottom leaves when they are 10 cm long. Let the top leaves continue growing.

For best harvests and to keep the leaves from going bitter, water during any early summer dry spells.

Mulching will help keep the soil cool, which is what this plant loves.

Additional Information

Treat it as you would spinach, cooking or eating raw. Mustard greens are also used in bio-remediation because they suck up contaminants and heavy metals in the soil; plants used for this purpose are not eaten but are disposed of in environmentally sound ways.

ONION

Onions for cooking or fresh use are best started early indoors to get a good jump on the season. They can be sown directly into the garden, but the crop will mature a little later.

When to Plant

The trick to sowing directly into the ground is to sow *early*. Seed that is not in the ground by the first week of May will not usually mature before frost.

But if you want to beat the season, sow indoors. Sow the seeds approximately .6 cm from each other, cover very lightly with soil, water with warm water, and give the seeds full sunlight. Grow them on with half-strength plant food and full light until the danger of heavy frost is over; then transplant.

If you want the really huge specialty onions such as Spanish onions, then I'd buy sets from a garden centre and plant these in late April.

Where to Plant

Plant in full sun in a well-drained, fertile soil.

How to Plant

If you want to sow outdoors, put the seeds 1 to 2 cm apart and .6 cm deep. Deep sowing will simply kill onion seed. Rows should be approximately 30 to 45 cm apart. You want to encourage air circulation in the garden to reduce or eliminate fungal problems.

Care & Maintenance

When the growing onions start to touch at this close spacing, thin and use any smaller, tender onions for cooking or pickling. This leaves the remaining onions adequate space to reach 5 to 7 cm in size.

Onions are a shallow-rooted vegetable so a liquid compost tea feeding early in the spring combined with a midsummer feeding of compost tea or liquid fish emulsion will give you excellent results. This is over and above the normal application of compost in the spring. Their shallow root systems also mean that you should not allow onions to get too dry during the heat of summer.

Harvest by thinning the plants as they mature.

Additional Information

There's a lot of advice about "knocking over" the tops of onions to make the bulbs grow larger. The reason you knock over the tops is to prevent heart rot if there is heavy rain just before you cure the bulbs. If there are no heavy rains forecast, and the bulb will not be absorbing excessive amounts of water, there is little reason to knock over the tops.

To cure the bulbs for storage, pull the onion bulbs out of the ground and allow them to sit on top of the soil for 7 to 10 days to "cure." Avoid leaving them exposed to frost. Leave the soil on the bulbs to dry out naturally. The neck will dry during this time and you can remove it and clean the bulbs just before storing them. (Necks are the long leaves that wither down when onions are pulled from the soil—you'll understand when you see them.) Do not cut into the green growth of the bulb before storage.

PARSNIP

Now this is one of those plants you either love or hate. I note that a bit of butter and brown sugar goes a long way toward improving the taste and that parsnips are incomparable when used in beef stews.

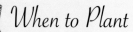

When to Plant

Parsnips are an early garden crop and the seed should be sown outdoors as soon as you can work your soil. Notice I said *seed*; no transplanting. At the very best of times, parsnip seed doesn't germinate well so follow my tips below.

Sowing a few radish seeds along with the parsnip seed would be helpful to mark the rows because this vegetable germinates slowly—you're looking at least three weeks before it will break the ground. And to make life interesting, if the weather turns back to really cold, or there are heavy frosts, or your ground dries out or crusts over, then it will take even longer or the seed will die and you'll have to resow.

Where to Plant

Plant in soil that is heavy in organic matter so it doesn't crust, and is deep so the plants grow well. You want a soil that is good for 30 cm down so the roots will grow straight and true. The requirements of parsnip are similar to carrot needs.

How to Plant

Sow seed .6 cm deep with one seed per centimetre. Once they germinate, thin to 5 to 7 cm between healthy seedlings. When you are weeding, hill up the shoulders of the parsnips to prevent a problem called "canker." Never stand too close to the row or you'll risk compacting the soil, which results in forked roots. Some gardeners lay down wooden planks between these rows to distribute their weight equally. Yes, this plant really is bothered that much by soil compaction.

Care & Maintenance

Overfertilizing will produce a range of problems such as divided roots, so compost rather than chemical fertilizer is the food of choice. A shovel of compost spread equally in a 15 cm band over the row should cover 1 to 1.5 metres of row.

Wait until after the first frost to harvest as cold weather and frosts increase the sugar content in the root. If you protect them from freezing by using a heavy mulch over the top of them, a parsnip can be left in the ground over winter. Harvest parsnips the first thing in the spring for great flavour.

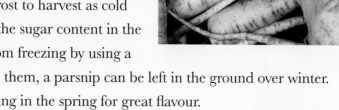

Additional Information

You may find caterpillars on your plants (swallowtail butterfly larva); handpicking and moving them to other plants is what the conservationists would suggest. But do remove them if you want a crop.

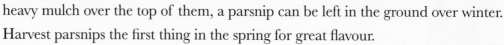

PEAS

I love fresh peas and these were a staple of my children's garden raiding for years. It's tough to be angry when your kids want to eat vegetables and harvest most of them for snacks.

When to Plant

Peas should be sown almost as early as you can work the soil; later plantings will simply not bear as heavily as the cold weather plantings. All you require is a soil temperature of 10°C and you're off and running. In my zone 5 garden, this occurs in early to mid-April in a decent year.

Normally, fall crops are sown in the first week of August.

Where to Plant

Plant in full sun. Peas benefit from a well-drained soil that is high in organic matter; adding compost to the soil is enough food for a fine pea crop.

How to Plant

Sow seed 2 to 3 cm deep (up or down a bit doesn't hurt) and cover. Later summer plantings can be sown even deeper at a depth of 3.5 cm to get steady moisture levels and be out of the direct heat of the sun.

Rows should be 1.5 to 1.8 m apart to allow for adequate air circulation.

Care & Maintenance

While you can let the vines ramble over the ground, the far better way is to drive stakes into the ground and string some form of support. A roll of plastic snow fence is ideal, or old diamond-wire fence from home fencing also works well. The top has to be supported with horizontal supports or you'll find the fencing leaning from the weight of the vines. Growing peas up a trellis or fence means harvesting is easier; you can see the pods. Air circulates around the vines and this keeps them much more disease free.

If you overfeed peas, you'll produce a lot of tender shoots, fewer flowers, and a ton of insects thanking you for the fine, tender lunch you've provided. Go easy on the feeding and use compost. Even commercial growers feed peas lightly as they produce their own nitrogen on root nodules.

Peas are shallow rooted so a steady supply of water applied via drip irrigation will pay off with large harvests of plump pods. Overhead irrigation during harvesting may increase problems like powdery mildew on crowded vines.

Also, because of their shallow root system, you have to be very careful of hoeing next to the rows; you'll have a tendency to chop off the feeder roots (never a good idea).

Additional Information

How much to plant? Well, 115 gms of seed will sow about 9 m of row; this will produce approximately 120 plants. Each plant should give you several dozen pods. Pick regularly as soon as they start to mature and the harvest will be extended. If you only pick once and then leave the vines alone, production will stop. Regular picking is the key to high yields.

Growing instructions are the same for edible podded peas as they are for shelling or dried peas.

PEPPER

Growing peppers in cooler climates always seems like a bit of a gamble to me. Some years the yield is great and other years I'm reminded that I live in a short-season climate. Here's what I've learned about growing this temperamental crop.

When to Plant

If you start your own peppers, sow the seed at the beginning of March or 10 to 12 weeks before you plan on planting them outdoors.

Seed likes to be kept at 21°C for germination, and use warm water to keep the soil temperatures high. Sow very thinly in a flat or pot. If you try crowding this plant, it will respond with fungus infections. Once there are four true leaves, transplant to their own pot or cell pack cell for growing on.

Grow the seedlings at 21°C days and 18°C nights and never let them get chilled or subsequent harvests will be low.

Where to Plant

Plant in full sunshine, in your most protected (and hence warmest) garden spot.

Peppers have a very fibrous root system and they perform best in well-aerated soils with high organic matter content. This is the long way of saying to save your best soils for your peppers.

How to Plant

After all danger of frost and the ground has warmed up (early June in zone 5), plant outside at 45 cm between plants and 76 cm between rows. A lot of folks rush this plant and can't figure out why they never get peppers.

Plant peppers up to the first set of leaves (the stem will root quite quickly, just like tomatoes), and avoid cold ground. Cool ground, with soil temperatures below 10°C, will guarantee a stunted plant and no pepper set.

Care & Maintenance

Soil temperatures above 29°C will also stunt the plant but we're not likely to see these unless the peppers are mulched under plastic. Excessive heat levels will build under plastic-mulched soils in our typical summer. If you use plastic to increase your spring soil temperatures, remove it by the end of June or whenever the soil starts to get too warm. An organic mulch of straw or leaves can be used in its place for the summer.

The single most important thing is to keep them continuously growing and not check their growth rate at all during the growing season. This means that those poor pepper transplants that are "on special" at the local plant sales depot are probably not a good bet if the roots are rootbound in their container.

Canadian researchers found that if they picked off the early flower buds on pepper plants, they got more peppers than if they left them on. It seems pepper does not set fruit like a tomato; that is, the earliest flowers are the earliest fruit. Instead, the pepper seems to ripen the crop all at the same time and then produces another set of flowers and peppers. If you pinch off the initial, lower flower buds, apparently the plant will set a more uniform flower set at the top of the plant and these will tend to ripen because the summer heat is perfect for their development.

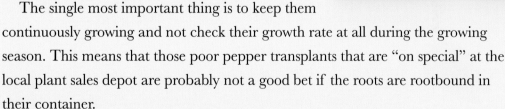

PEPPER *continued*

Alternately, you can dig a trench in the garden about 18 cm deep, work in compost, and plant in the bottom of the trench. Cover the trench with a row cover to help keep the heat in the trench. This trench growing removes the pepper from cool temperatures and drying winds and gives it a perfect environment for establishment in cool-garden areas.

Also, you can simply use row covers to hold the spring heat in and protect the plants against cool nights. You can also protect the plants from fall frosts this way. Row covers are the simplest solution to getting good pepper crops.

Avoid excess nitrogen when growing peppers; this produces large plants with no fruit. The solution is to use compost as a source of food instead of chemical fertilizers. Digging in compost .6 to 1 cm deep will solve this problem as well as adding the necessary organic matter. Also apply several applications of fish emulsion during the summer months to solve any low phosphorus level problems the plant may be experiencing.

Additional Information

Peppers really grow too slowly to start them directly into the soil anywhere but in the warmest of climates.

I grow two kinds of peppers in my gardens: hot peppers and sweet peppers. The difference between the two is found in the level of capsaicinoids that exist within the fruit. Fruit that are relatively low in these compounds are considered to be a sweet pepper while fruit that have higher concentrations are considered to be hot.

This chemical, capsaicinoid, is a powerful fungicide and the pepper seed produces it in a biological adaptation to protect itself from fungal attacks during its long germination phase.

It is also interesting to note that all peppers produce these capsaicinoids, but only after 20 days on the bush and then in varying amounts depending on the variety, the heat units in the garden, and soil moisture measurements.

The hotter and drier the season, the more powerful the "heat" produced by the peppers. This is one reason that even a sweet pepper may become bitter if it's stressed during its ripening stage; they too are producing the chemical capsaicinoid in their seeds.

Another note to clear up a common question: red peppers are simply mature peppers. All peppers will turn red (more or less depending on the variety) if left on the bush to mature.

Another common misconception relates to the "days to maturity" rating found on peppers (and tomatoes). This rating measures the time taken for ripening fruit from the day of transplanting given a standard set of sunlight values. It is itself variable; if we have a hotter or cooler summer than the standard measurements, the days to maturity will change accordingly. This may allow some gardeners with hot, protected gardens to grow peppers to maturity that have longer seasons than I can with my open, exposed garden. This is an example of microclimates changing growing patterns in gardens.

POLE BEAN

Pole beans can be quite useful in the garden; you can use them as a fast-growing hedge that will climb up to cover a trellis or fence, or use the beans for fresh eating, and the flowers are quite attractive in their own right. A climber for privacy that provides both veggies and flowers for the gardener—what more can you ask for?

When to Plant

Plant after the ground has warmed up in mid- to late May.

Where to Plant

It does best in full sun, well-drained locations, and a soil high in compost. If you haven't graduated to organic gardening yet but insist on using chemical fertilizers, do so very carefully on pole beans. While other vegetables can handle a little too much fertilizer, pole beans will simply burn up.

How to Plant

Plant seed 1.5 to 2 cm deep. Plant 5 to 6 beans in each 30-cm-wide hill, but when they germinate and start to grow, thin the hill to the 3 strongest plants.

If you try to grow too many plants in too small a supporting system, they'll strangle each other instead of producing beans (this plant has never learned how to play with its closest neighbours). If you try to grow them on the ground, they will wind around each other in a form of plant wrestling that will see them choke each other to death.

Care & Maintenance

Harvest the pods when they are still young and tender; a mature bean pod is a ferocious thing to try to eat. You should get a harvest at least once a week for about six weeks before the frost takes them out.

Finally, when frost is threatening, go out and rip-harvest your beans. Pull up the vines and take every bean (including all the babies). The small beans are quite edible and tender and it is far easier to take down bean plants when they are still green and alive than when they're hit by frost and rather messy and wilted.

Additional Information

How much seed should you plant? Well, figure that a hill contains 3 plants. Fifty to 60 gms of seed will give you approximately 25 hills.

Estimate .45 kg of harvested beans per hill. Maybe a bit more, maybe a bit less depending on the season, fertility levels, and the amount of rain you get.

Keep the support to a height you can harvest. By August, the beans should be up to the top of a 1.8 m pole and hanging down over the tops. If you give them taller supports, harvesting becomes a bit of a problem.

As with many other garden vegetables, it is generally recommended that you not weed pole beans when the plants are wet or when the dew is still on the plants as this encourages the spread of disease. Wait until the sun dries things off to work your plants.

PUMPKIN

Growing pumpkins for Halloween or Thanksgiving pies is pretty basic gardening. Remember that this is just a big squash plant and you'll be fine.

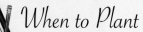

When to Plant

For good size fruit, start the seed indoors in 10 cm pots the first week of May. Plant two seeds per pot and thin to the most vigorous. Keep the soil temperatures at 21°C to germinate and then grow on at 15.5°C for thick, sturdy stems. Feed lightly with half-strength fish emulsion on a weekly basis.

If you are not interested in huge pumpkins or large crops, then you can direct sow the seed at the end of May when the ground warms up. Plant 2 seeds every 30 cm and thin out to 1 plant (the strongest) every 60 cm apart in the row. If you are growing in hills of 1.5 m in diameter, go with 2 plants per hill.

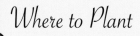

Where to Plant

Plant in full, hot sun in well-drained, fertile soils.

How to Plant

Transplant into a sunny spot leaving approximately 1.5 to 2.5 m between plants. A giant pumpkin will require a 4.5-m-diameter circle to grow in.

Care & Maintenance

Never let pumpkins wilt or stop growing as this will check the size of the fruit. They love compost and organic matter. In the spring before planting, work as much as you can into the basic planting area and then be prepared for a weekly fish emulsion and/or compost tea feeding every week during the growing season.

Try not to wet the leaves when you water this plant; you may run into mildew problems if the leaves are kept wet.

Harvest the fruit when the skins are bright orange and hard. Harvest before a hard frost as frost will degrade the skin and it will start to rot. If there is no hard frost, the fruit can be left on the vine right up to Halloween. Leave a few centimetres of stem on the pumpkin if you're going to try to store it.

Additional Information

A pumpkin will keep producing fruit right up to frost because it produces both male and female flowers on each vine. If you want really large fruit, the trick is to wait until you see the fruit reaching the size of baseballs on regular plants (the size of volleyballs on giant pumpkin seed) and then leave only three fruits closest to the vine planting spot; cut off any fruit that are developed farther out on the vines. Do not disturb the leaves; we need them to produce energy for the main plant and the three fruits you'll leave. If you want to produce the biggest fruit possible, only leave one pumpkin on each vine. Remove all flowers as they grow and prune off any fruit you miss.

RADISH

Radishes are so easy to grow it is almost criminal to suggest that you read an entire page about how to grow them.

When to Plant

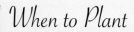

Sow in the spring as soon as you can work the ground. The seed will germinate and be up out of the ground in about five days. Don't worry about frost, snow, or cold; heavy freezing will hurt them but that's about it. Sow a new crop every week until it starts to get too hot; they do not like hot weather.

Where to Plant

Plant in full sun to part shade in almost any soil for spring crops, but you'll need good, well-drained soils for the main season and fall crops.

How to Plant

Sow the seed about .6 to .75 cm deep at 1 seed per centimetre of row. Thin the resulting seedlings so they are around 3 to 4 cm apart.

This means that the rows should be very short because (think about it) how many radishes can you really eat in salads or stir-fries?

Care & Maintenance

Harvest radishes regularly because they really are only in prime condition for a few days, it seems. To keep them mild tasting—not blazing hot and tough—you need to grow them quickly. Think lots of compost in the top few centimetres of soil (they are shallow rooted) and absolutely no moisture stress (keep them well watered). If you let them dry out or get too hot in July and August, they'll quickly become woody and not nice to eat.

Additional Information

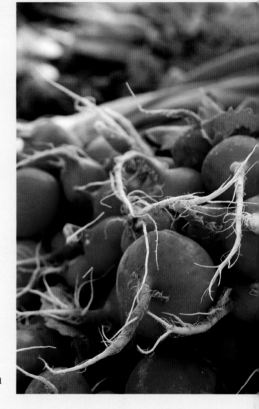

You may find when trying to grow radishes in the middle of the summer that the long days and high temperatures make them go to flower very quickly. This is to be expected. Just yank them out and compost them.

Because they are shallow rooted, cultivate as shallowly as you can. Use compost in the soil because radishes do not like overfeeding. Overfeeding attracts root maggots (they like the extra nitrogen in the soil and root).

Use radishes as row markers for other plants such as carrots or tuck a few here and there between tomato plants. Use any "wasted space" in the garden to grow them rather than give them their own row.

SPINACH

Spinach is an extremely fast-growing and easy crop for early, cool spring weather. It can be one of your first homegrown greens to lead off salad season.

When to Plant

The nice thing about spinach is the seed germinates better in cold ground (it prefers soil temperatures of 4°C) rather than the higher temperatures later in the spring or summer.

Later sowings will sprout faster but have a reduced germination rate. This means you'll get the seedlings earlier but fewer of them will sprout for the amount of seed you sow.

Generally, as soon as you can walk on your garden soil, you can plant spinach seed. That's about early April in zones 4 to 5—or as soon as the frost is out of the picture. Sow a short row every week until the middle of June for a reliable supply. Don't bother sowing after June or when the weather gets really warm as spinach doesn't stay in "leaf" form; instead it bolts up into flower and produces unusable leaves. Whether it is the warm temperatures or the longer days with increasing sunlight, spinach doesn't do well in the heat.

Where to Plant

Plant in full sun in early spring; the location can be in light shade in late spring or early summer to see if you can extend your harvest. Slightly shaded areas will stay cooler longer in the summer. Any garden soil except heavy clay is fine for this vegetable.

How to Plant

Sow your seed 1.2 cm deep and about 1 seed to the centimeter. You're going to thin excess plants so the mature spinach plants are 20 cm apart or just touching leaves. Keep harvesting and using the thinnings as you thin plants to the 20-cm spacing. After that, harvest as many of the outer leaves as you need. If you've sown too many plants for use, harvest the entire plant and use those very tender inner leaves.

You can resow again in early September for later crops and you'll find spinach to be reasonably frost hardy, giving you fresh greens right up until a very hard freeze. You'll find you get a first harvest about 45 days after sowing.

Care & Maintenance

You're not going to let spinach plants get fully mature; although a mature plant will get larger than 30 cm tall, by the time it is ready to do so, you're already moving onto other greens and pulling these spinach plants out. When spinach matures, it will be ready to "bolt" and set seed.

Additional Information

Not too many pests bother spinach, although you may find a few aphids trying to hitch a ride. A quick jet of water takes care of this problem.

SUMMER SQUASH

When we talk the squash family, we're talking about the squash that do not store well and should be eaten fresh. Zucchini, butter crookneck, marrows, spaghetti, and scallop types of squash plants are all grown in similar ways. And if you harvest them regularly, they'll keep producing all summer.

When to Plant

Plant after all danger of frost has passed and the ground is warm enough to put your wrist into the soil without feeling uncomfortable. The seeds rot quickly in cold ground and you'll do better if you wait a bit with this plant.

Where to Plant

Plant in full sun in good soil.

How to Plant

These plants are so easy to grow from seed that you should never consider purchasing started plants. Sow after the ground has truly warmed up. Sow 1 seed every 6 to 7 centimetres of row and approximately 1.5 cm deep. The rows should be 1.2 m apart if you're growing a lot. Mind you, two zucchini plants are enough for an average-sized invading army, so why anybody would want a row of them is beyond me. Seriously folks, you'll get a squash a day from two plants.

Care & Maintenance

If you grow them in hills (slightly raised piles of soil approximately 45 cm across), you can put 4 seeds in a hill. Construct your hills 1 m apart in all directions. Thin to only 2 seeds in a hill and pick the strongest seedlings to leave when the seedlings reach 5 to 7 cm tall.

Summer squash really like even moisture (they don't appreciate drying out) and soil that has been enriched with organic matter. Adding compost heavily to this section of the garden will almost guarantee a good return. You'll also find that adding a mulch around the plants in July will even out the moisture levels and keep the soil at a steady temperature to increase your yields.

Additional Information

Harvest when they're small, in the 10- to 15-cm-long range, and not when they are gigantic. Those pictures you see of huge fruit in the seed catalogs are generally woody and not worth the eating (even my squash-eating buddies won't eat those).

You may find squash bugs and cucumber beetles chowing down on the leaves and these pests can defoliate squash plants almost overnight. While it is a good idea *not* to spray during flowering (you kill off their predators as well), a dusting of rotenone or diatomaceous earth will slow them down. Handpicking is a very useful exercise as you're sure to see and find a ton of pests (drop them into a bucket of soapy water to drown). Note that squash bugs hang around overnight in flowers that have bloomed and closed that day; now you know where to look.

And remember, the more fruit you pick, the more you get.

SWISS CHARD

Swiss chard is always sown outdoors. I guess you could do it inside if you wanted to, but why bother when it is so easy to grow in the garden?

When to Plant

Sow outside as soon as the ground can be worked safely (without compacting the soil) and sow every two weeks from mid-April until mid-June. After this, it starts to get too hot to really grow this kind of leafy vegetable (the leaves will get bitter).

Replant in the late summer when the nights start to cool down for fall crops or treat as noted under "Care & Maintenance."

Where to Plant

Plant in full sun to very light shade in the heat of the summer in a well-drained soil. It will grow in almost any soil except for swamps. However, it does prefer good garden soil.

How to Plant

Sow seed 1.2 cm deep and several seeds to the centimeter. Thin the seedlings when they are 5 cm tall and leave spacing at 10 cm apart. Use the thinnings in salads as they are quite tender.

When the remaining plants start to touch each other, pull every second one so the final spacing is a plant every 20 cm. I usually pull them as they mature when the leaves just start to touch, and pick the smaller of the two so I'm always pulling out the weaker plant (and eating it). I don't have a system, but rather I go down the row and look for smaller plants that are being dwarfed by nearby plants. These get eaten first.

Care & Maintenance

In early August, trim off all the browning or poor-looking leaves and apply a liquid fish emulsion fertilizer. The boost in performance will give a lot of new, fresh growth that you can harvest for the rest of the summer right up until a snowfall knocks off the plants. They are very hardy and will bear right through all early frosts.

Water this plant right through the heat of the summer. If you neglect to water it, you'll find the central stalk will go "woody" and will stop producing new and succulent growth.

Additional Information

You'll find that the different leaves have different tastes (the inner ones are more tender and the outer ones are fantastic in stir-fries).

Swiss chard is a good alternative to spinach because it tends to continue producing right through the heat of the summer if watered, whereas spinach does not grow well in the heat. And Swiss chard resists bolting much better than spinach.

Problems are the same as any of the cabbage family. Watch for green cabbage worms all summer and aphids on early plants.

TOMATILLO

Tomatillo is used in some garden writing to refer to two different plants. Sometimes it refers to *Physalis philadelphica* and sometimes to *Physalis peruviana*. The culture and care of these plants is the same although the *P. peruviana* fruit (also known as Ground Cherry) is smaller and sweeter. I could tell you how I rarely see the sweet fruit because they mysteriously disappear when my partner does some weeding but that might not be the smartest thing to do.

When to Plant

Start seed indoors in early April for a late May outdoor planting. Grow several seeds per pot and thin to the largest and strongest before transplanting outdoors. Direct sowing in the garden at the end of May will give you a harvest in mid-September in zone 5. You'll get a harvest mid- to the end of September in a zone 4 garden, but any colder than that and you should start them indoors.

Where to Plant

Tomatillos do best in full sun or very light shade in an average soil. They seem to grow darn near anywhere and they will self-sow in a zone 4 or warmer garden. This is a robust, spreading plant (upwards of a metre) so give it room to spread.

How to Plant

Treat tomatillos like a tomato for the best results. Sow and barely cover the seed, keeping the soil temperature at 21°C. They should sprout in 10 days. After 5 weeks (or when a plant develops 4 true leaves) transplant to its own pot or thin to 1 per pot and grow in a strong light. Only water with luke-warm water.

Transplant outdoors after all danger of frost.

This plant requires two of itself to set fruit; they are not generally self-fruitful so plan on having two growing side-by-side in the garden.

Tomatillo is a large plant that turns into a small bush if grown properly. Space 50 cm apart if you need to crowd them, or 1 m if you don't. They will grow to 40 cm tall.

Care & Maintenance

There is very little care needed for this plant. There is no staking or pruning required. Watch for aphids (wash them off with a strong jet of water) and that's about the extent of damage.

Just keep the weeds away from the plant so you can find the fruit when it matures.

The fruit is ripe when the husks turn brown and split open. The small fruit will simply cover a well-grown plant. The very seedy fruit is sweet enough to eat on its own.

Additional Information

The large fruit is a mainstay of Mexican cooking, while the small sweet fruit is amazing in desserts.

The plant is a member of the nightshade family (like the tomato) and no other parts of the plant should be eaten.

TOMATO

The tomato is the single most popular vegetable that is grown in the organic gardening circle. Heck, it's the most popular vegetable grown in the home vegetable garden. Period.

When to Plant

Sow seed indoors. Calculate eight weeks back from your last frost date and sow your seed then. I put my transplants outdoors in mid-May, so I'd plant the second week of March. If you sow earlier than eight weeks, your seedlings will be long and lanky and stretched-out ugly.

Where to Plant

Plant in full sun in a fertile, well-drained soil. Your basic great gardening soil that only exists in writers' imaginations. Give tomatoes your best location and add as much compost as you can.

How to Plant

The easiest thing for home gardeners to do is sow seeds directly into small pots of artificial soil.

Figure two seeds per pot (and thin the seedlings to the strongest one after three weeks). Grow as many pots as you need plants. This will give the transplant enough room to grow to develop a thick top and full root system. A plant that has been grown in its own pot will not suffer transplant shock when it is moved to the garden. Giving adequate space is particularly important if you do not have full outdoor light levels with a greenhouse or large grow light system. Crowded seedlings tend to be long and thin.

If you need *a lot* of seedlings, you can sow them in a flat by keeping the seeds approximately 2 to 3 cm apart. Then transplant them into growing cells. The problem here is that unless you have adequate light levels you will produce inferior transplants.

The soil temperature for germinating tomato seed should be around 23°C. Use a heating cable or mat to produce this heat because inadequate room temperatures will only produce sporadic germination.

When seedlings break the soil around the 10-day mark, reduce the temperature to 18°C. When they have 4 true leaves, reduce the temperature again and grow on at 15°C.

Feed seedlings once or twice a week with a quarter-strength fish emulsion.

Staked plants can be grown on 30- to 45-cm centers with rows 1 m apart. The rule of thumb is that each tomato needs 900 sq. cm of growing space if you're growing them straight up.

Sprawling plants should be put into the full sunshine at 60- to 75-cm spacing. The rows should be 1.25 to 1.5 m apart. Tomatoes can really spread.

Care & Maintenance

After all danger of frost has passed, transplant outdoors. "Harden off" your transplants before planting; I usually put mine outdoors during the day and indoors at night for a week before I put them in the ground. This gets them used to high light levels, the wind, and the vagaries of the garden before being left to fend for themselves.

TOMATO *continued*

If your transplants are too long and leggy, harden off, dig a trench 15 cm deep, and lay the transplant into the trench so only the top 15 cm of the plant is showing at the end of the trench.

Cover the entire stem (leaving only the top 15 cm above ground) and the stem will root. This eliminates weak growth and prevents the plant from flopping around like a fish out of water in every breeze.

As my tomatoes grow up the stakes, I tie them to the stake every 15 cm with binder twine.

Any thick twine or old pantyhose will do well. You simply want to avoid cutting into the stem with thin ties. I pick a single leader (a single stem) to train to a stake and I remove all other branches. You'll often see a "sucker" trying to grow between the stem and a big leaf. Pinch all these suckers off and only allow the main stem to grow.

Is there special care needed if I let my plants sprawl? No. Just plant, water, feed, take care of pests, and harvest. Pretty simple, really.

 ## Additional Information

Remember that cool nights deform fruit, so delaying planting until the nights are warm will please tomatoes.

One of the most basic decisions is whether to grow determinate or indeterminate tomato plants. Determinate plants are bush types on which a majority of the fruit will ripen within a very few days. All the tomatoes ripen—bang!—all at once. This is great if you are using them for canning or freezing or processing them in some way. There will be a few stragglers coming along after the main harvest but the bulk of the crop will ripen together. This kind of growth is best suited for sprawling plant growing.

Indeterminate plants ripen in a sequence. The first fruit set ripens before the second set; each set lower down on the stem ripens before the next higher one. This kind of growth is best suited for staking and fresh eating. This plant will continue to ripen and set fruit until frost knocks on your garden door.

Before you plant your tomatoes, ask yourself whether you have an abundance of garden space to let them sprawl or if your space is restricted so you'll have to

stake them. Sprawling plants yield more per plant, but staked fruit yield more per square foot of garden space (you can crowd tomatoes a bit when staking).

Cages are an intermediate form of staking and, quite frankly, I don't think they give the benefits of either. They have their proponents but I'm not one of them. I either like the anarchy of the sprawling patch or the tightly controlled growing habits of a staked and pruned plant. If you use cages, set your cages deeply into the garden soil; a fully grown tomato plant can easily pull small cages over.

Determinate plants do much better when left to sprawl or when grown in cages, and indeterminate plants do better when staked.

TURNIP

Turnips were a staple plant of the pioneers, as they were an easy crop to grow in almost any weather or soil. People and animals ate them through the worst of times in building our country. But ever since, their reputation as a nutritious and versatile vegetable has suffered. Mind you, it may be because of the way this plant has been overcooked, mashed, and mixed into any number of bland recipes.

When to Plant

Sow seed when the soil temperatures reach 15°C, normally mid- to late May.

If you plant more than one row, the rows should be 60 to 75 cm apart. You can sow as late as the last two weeks in June to get fall crops and it is these fall crops that will grow larger and more reliably than the earlier sowings.

Where to Plant

Plant in full sunshine in well-drained soils.

How to Plant

Sow seed 1 to 2 cm deep at approximately 1 seed to a centimeter and thin out the seedlings to 1 every 15 cm when the plants are 7 cm tall.

Note that a few too many seeds or too few seeds isn't a major problem. You're going to be thinning them out (the greens are quite edible) as they mature, so you only have mature plants in proper spacing.

Care & Maintenance

Turnips are a pretty pest- and disease-free crop. You might see black rot or black leg (rotting) if you've planted turnips or cabbage family crops in the same space in the preceding 2 to 3 years. This is a great crop to rotate around. For the same reason, do not work around the plants when they have wet leaves (this is a pretty common recommendation for all garden plants). Remove all turnips from the garden in the fall and do not leave any to rot over the winter as this will encourage the development of rotting problems in your soil.

Harvesting roots is as simple as digging them up and washing them well with clean water. Avoid any dirt on the root to store them properly. Dry the roots, trim off the leaves, and store at 1° to 2°C just above freezing with high humidity and they'll keep for 4 to 6 months. Waxing them will help with storage. There's no need to buff the wax, though.

Additional Information

Turnips, or rutabaga as they are more properly known, are grown from seed (not transplants) and are specific in what they like. For example, they don't like fresh manure (it leads to high nitrogen levels that cause poor storage and taste), or high doses of chemical fertilizer for the same reason. Compost is a great food for this root crop.

Sometimes flea beetles eat the leaves; a dusting of diatomaceous earth pretty much takes care of this problem.

WATERMELON

The main trick to being successful with watermelons is to choose early varieties. If you pick a larger, long-day variety, you'll still be waiting for fruit to ripen when the snow is on the ground.

When to Plant

Start your seed indoors in the middle of April. Do not sow after the first of May as the crop won't have time to ripen.

Where to Plant

Plant in full sun in rich, well-drained soils.

How to Plant

Watermelons do not like to have their roots disturbed so transplant *carefully*.

Each seed needs its own pot because you don't want to disturb the roots when you transplant. Use 2 to 3 seeds to each 10-cm pot because you'll thin out the weakest seedlings once the plant gets to the 3-leaf stage (3 true leaves, not counting the first tiny seedling leaves).

Soil temperature is critical for success with watermelons. Ensure the soil is at least 22° to 23°C. Only use lukewarm water on the seedlings—never use cold water. If you lower the soil temperature with cold water, the seeds will not be happy and will not germinate.

Once the seeds are up, grow them at an air temperature of 22° to 23°C with good air circulation and high light levels. Feed weekly with half-strength fish emulsion to keep the seedlings growing.

Harden melon transplants off before you put them outdoors. If you move them directly from the higher heat indoors to outside temperatures, you'll stunt them and set them back.

Put the melons outside after all danger of frost has passed and when the soil has warmed up. In my zone 4 to 5 garden, this is normally the middle of June. You can stretch black plastic mulch (garbage bags work well) over the planting area to warm it up as soon as the ground is workable. Then, when the air temperatures are high enough, the soil under the black poly will be quite warm enough for melons. Weight the plastic edges so they don't fly away in the wind. Some gardeners leave the black plastic in place for this crop and merely make a slit in the plastic to plant a potted watermelon into the ground under the poly.

Care & Maintenance

Once planted, remember that watermelons are mostly water and you have to provide them with enough to grow both the vines and fruits. They are also very shallow-rooted plants and weeding next to the vine has to be done carefully or you'll chop up the roots. So, don't move the vines; they resent this big time.

Feed compost tea and/or fish emulsion every few weeks to keep watermelons healthy and growing.

Additional Information

Once they are large, how do you know they're ripe? Look at the rind on the bottom of the watermelon as it turns from white to pale yellow. Pale yellow means this baby is done. You can figure you'll realistically get three melons from each vine.

WINTER SQUASH

Winter squash is one of the vegetables I've never managed to like. I used to grow all kinds of them for the family and, even though the growing was easy, the eating was not (for me). I do know that baked squash with butter and a touch of brown sugar is a staple in the fall. But many people love them, so I include it here.

When to Plant

Sow the seed of all winter squash the first week of June in zone 5. Warmer zones can bump this up a week or two while colder zones should delay planting until the ground is warm enough. See page 19 for how to judge. This ensures the soil temperatures are high enough for good germination and that the plant flowers later after cool nights are over. Cool nights prevent good pollination.

Where to Plant

All squashes grow much better in full sun, in a well-drained, fertile soil. Heavy clay or waterlogged soils will rot either the roots or the ripening squash, or both.

How to Plant

Plant in small hills at 4 seeds per hill. The hills should be 1 to 2 m apart. Plant the seed approximately 1.2 cm deep and firm the soil on top of the seed to ensure it is in contact with soil (not air).

Care & Maintenance

Remember that a squash plant is a shallow-rooted plant so weed quite carefully when using a hoe to avoid cutting off feeder roots. Do not allow winter squash to fully dry out in drought or you'll reduce your harvest.

Harvest before the first frost and allow the fruit to ripen outside for a week or two to harden up the skins. Without this curing outdoors, the squash might not overwinter very well. DO NOT TRY TO STORE UNRIPE FRUIT. Contrary to popular belief, fruit that has been heavily frosted will not store well, either.

Additional Information

Store squash in a warmish 15°C, dry space. Treat them gently to avoid bruising and, if you can, leave a space between fruits for the air to circulate to stop any mold from developing.

The only pest of major consequence is the squash bug. You can use rotenone, diatomaceous earth, or handpicking to control them.

A question that often comes up is that the plant is producing lots of flowers but has no fruit. Causes for this are that the temperatures are too cold for pollen to be viable, honeybees are not flying to yellow flowers yet but are focusing on other colours, or that the plant is still only producing one sex of flower. This is one reason we like to grow many plants, so there is a better chance of pollination. The remedy is always to relax and wait; there's not much else you can do.

Wow! And they say kids don't like veggies ... they do if they can help grow them.

HERBS

✦

Every vegetable garden needs a few culinary kitchen herbs to spice up the salads and for adding incredible flavour to foods. There are two bits of advice I normally give (and practice myself). The first is to locate the herb and vegetable garden as close to the kitchen door as possible so you can easily grab a few leaves or plants for whatever culinary delight you're creating. The second is to grow what you'll use; restrict yourself (for at least the first few years) to those kitchen herbs you currently love to cook with. Expand your experimental herb garden as you tackle more recipes.

The basics you need to really make your herb garden complete follow. Many of these plants fit nicely into the crop rotation schedules discussed earlier in the book. Some, like arugula, are perfect for early crops that will be followed by later heat-loving plants such as peppers.

Bon appétit!

ARUGULA

Also known as roquette or rocket, this is a tough, annual leafy green plant with a zing to it. If you want a peppery taste in salads, then plan on growing this herb. The one caution with this plant is that during hot weather or with older plants, the leaves get quite bitter. I suspect you're not going to like a bitter-pepper taste in your salads.

When to Plant

In spring, sow with peas and other early crops. Sow every two weeks until late June; any later plantings are going to become bitter in the heat. For a fall garden, start planting every two weeks again in late August or early September or whenever the nights become cool. This is a seasonal plant and you'll be able to start sowing earlier in the North than you will in southern Ontario. Cool nights are the key here. A well-established arugula plant will often survive the winter in a zone 4 garden so don't pull them up in the fall cleanup. You'll be able to get an early spring crop if it does survive, and be able to harvest in April and early May (about the same time as dandelions bloom in your neighbourhood).

Where to Plant

Plant in full sun, in decent soils. Arugula will not overwinter in clay soil.

How to Plant

Sow seed 1 cm deep and keep the soil damp.

Care & Maintenance

This is a fast-growing, leafy plant that should give you a harvest 6 weeks after sowing. You can harvest the outer leaves or dig up the entire plant depending on how much "pepper" you want in your salad.

Additional Information

Most people sow way too much arugula given that a few leaves go a long way in a salad. You are much better off to sow 3 to 6 plants every week than try to grow several dozen plants at one time. After the plants mature, they start going bitter so you want to keep young plants constantly growing.

As you harvest the tender outer leaves, more will be produced. Harvest until the peppery taste becomes too bitter or the next crop is maturing. Taste before adding to a salad! A little bit of arugula goes a long way.

At some point, it might produce flowers. These, too, are edible.

When the plant becomes too bitter to eat, pull it out and plant something else, like a fast crop of lettuce, in its place.

BASIL

Sweet basil is a must-grow if you like tomatoes. They are a perfect combination and you owe it to yourself to keep a steady supply coming along in the kitchen garden. I simply can't imagine not having one of the many varieties of sweet basil available in my kitchen.

When to Plant

Sow indoors six weeks before you want to plant outside. In my zone 4 to 5 garden, this usually means I'm sowing in early April for a mid- to late May outdoor transplanting.

Otherwise, sow outdoors in early June when the soil is good and warm.

Where to Plant

Plant in full sunshine or very light shade, in a decent soil. Basil doesn't like heavy clay all that much.

How to Plant

Sow seed .3 cm deep, just barely covering it, and keep the soil temperature at 18°C minimum. They should start germinating in 6 to 8 days.

Plant outdoors (or thin direct sown plants to 30 cm apart).

Outdoor plants should be sown at the same depth and thinned out starting when they are about 2 to 3 cm tall. Eat the thinnings.

Care & Maintenance

Do not crowd basil or you'll find it quickly succumbs to stem rot (blackened stems) and withering or slow growth problems. Give it lots of air circulation. This is why it is important to sow the seed at least 1 to 2 cm apart when seeding both indoors and outdoors and then transplanting or thinning as soon as the plants are 2 to 3 cm tall.

Harvest top growth by cutting or pinching off the new tender growth. Keep doing this all summer long to keep the plant producing new tender growth. Pinch off flowers as they are produced so the plant's energy will go toward producing more leaves rather than flowers.

Additional Information

Basil is wonderful in salad dressings, with any tomato dish, or even with chicken stuffing. This is a frost-tender annual plant but it can be dug up, potted before fall frost, and protected for an extra month or two in a sunny windowsill. It does get sparse and leggy during the winter and I normally toss mine to the compost pile when this happens.

Red-leaved varieties and dwarf varieties of sweet basil are all quite edible. However, do not expect to eat plants such as holy basil or camphor basil unless you have a very different sense of taste (these are grown for fragrance rather than culinary uses). My favourites are the large-leaved varieties that give me large garden plants *and* big harvests.

CHIVES

Chives have a mild onion taste, are easy to grow, and will likely turn into a weed in your garden. It is a hardy plant right up to zone 3.

When to Plant

Sow seed inside in mid-February. Plant in 10-cm pots where they can be grown from seed to adult plants before you transplant the entire pot outdoors after all danger of frost.

Where to Plant

As a member of the onion family, chives should be planted in full sun to very light shade in a sandier soil. Heavy clay will rot over-wintering bulbs.

How to Plant

Indoors, sow individual seeds 1 cm apart and .6 cm deep. Firm the soil around the seed so damp soil is in contact with the seed. Keep the soil temperature at 20°C for good germination percentage. Water with lukewarm water and you should see small, hairlike growth in 12 to 14 days.

Outdoors, transplant clumps into the garden and space 20 cm apart. Unless you want to grow them one year and start harvesting the second, do not direct-sow chives because they are such a slow grower. This plant will self-sow once it starts producing flowers.

Care & Maintenance

Very little care is needed. Cut flowers off (they'll make excellent chive vinegar) so they don't self-sow and become a weed.

Some gardeners cut the entire clump to the ground after blooming. The plant will resprout and produce tender, spearlike leaves. If you harvest more than a few spears every now and then, you will have to toss an extra shovel of compost around this plant. Too much harvesting (repeated cutting to the ground) will weaken it.

Divide the mature clumps every few years to keep them healthy and growing well. You can divide large clumps in the spring or fall to increase the number of plants.

Additional Information

'Profusion' is a chive variety that doesn't produce seeds. Divide it to obtain more plants.

Garlic chives is another member of the onion family that has a garlicky-onion taste and is excellent in the garden. I wouldn't have a garden without this easily grown plant. Treat it exactly like regular chives. The flowers are white (regular chives are light purple) and the leaves are flat (regular chive leaves are tubular), but grow them the same.

DILL

My kids turned into dill-pickle fanatics early in life. They taste-tested and evaluated ferociously with every new batch of dill pickles and have even been known to "test" an entire jar at one sitting just to make sure that each pickle was up to the standard. You had to be fast in our house to get your share.

When to Plant

Direct sow dill seed in mid-May in zones 4 to 5, or when the ground has warmed up. A soil temperature less than 16°C is going to stop germination and the seed will rot.

Where to Plant

A good sunny and warm spot is ideal. You are going to want your hottest garden spot for dill because it needs to mature and set seed before fall if you want those great dill pickles.

The fun thing about dill is that it isn't fussy about sandy or clay soils. It will adapt to almost anything it finds itself growing in; you have no excuse not to try this plant.

How to Plant

Plant .6 cm deep and barely cover the seed. Firm to make sure the soil is in contact with the seed. Keep the soil damp. Sow at 2 seeds per 2 to 3 cm or so.

Do not sow indoors or try to transplant because this plant is "miffy."

Miffy is a grower's word for "maybe-iffy," something that doesn't like to be transplanted or grown easily.

Care & Maintenance

Thin garden seedlings to 10 to 15 cm apart when they are 5 to 8 cm tall. This is all the space they need to grow into mature plants (in about 70 days).

You might want to sow several times every two weeks just to make sure you have a good stand and that you're going to hit the weather window so the plants set seeds. With several plantings, you're also going to have a fresh supply of tender young leaves for salads right through the summer.

Additional Information

A mature dill plant is going to be about 1 m tall and quite attractive with flowers resembling Queen Anne's lace.

The stalks are a darker blue-green tone and are very pungent tasting. I'm told by the pickle fans in the family that the seeds and flower parts are what they recommend for pickle making; the stems should be discarded. The tender leaves grace salads throughout the summer.

You can also cut the stems and hang them upside-down in a dry place to store until you need them.

OREGANO

Oregano is too often sold as a perennial when in fact it is a tender-perennial in most gardens colder than zone 5. The ornamental forms of this plant are tender even in my warmer zone 5 garden area, particularly in a year without snow cover during those regularly scheduled minus-40 degree January days.

When to Plant

In any garden from zone 5 and colder, this plant is an indoor starter if you want a harvest. I routinely start it in mid-January to get a good-sized clump by the Victoria Day Weekend but you can start your own as late as March 1 and still get a harvest. Transplant outdoors after all danger of frost has passed; do not disturb the tender roots at all. The option is to buy a started plant in the spring if your existing overwintered plant looks dead.

Where to Plant

Plant in full sun in soil with good drainage. Clay soil, shade, or too wet conditions are going to lead to winterkill. I used to grow mine in a sunny rock garden where it thrived most years.

How to Plant

Oregano is a poor germinator so if you get 60 percent of the seeds to sprout, you're doing well. Put 6 to 10 seeds in a 10-cm pot and keep the soil temperature at normal room temperatures.

Do not cover the seed. Simply press the seed into the soil and water with lukewarm water. Seed will take three weeks or more to germinate.

Care & Maintenance

Keep the plants well trimmed and harvest the young growing shoots until midsummer. This "thickens up" the plant and prevents it from setting flowers. After midsummer, don't harvest anymore and allow the plant to store energy for winter survival.

Additional Information

If you are determined to try an outdoor sowing, let me suggest you time it so that you're sowing right about the time the dandelions are finishing blooming. This should give you the soil temperature oregano needs.

Oregano sends out runners and these can be divided in their second year (divide plants every two to three years). One trick to keeping the plant surviving is to divide regularly and always keep young and thriving plants. Older oregano plants tend to lose vigour.

There are "discussions" (a polite way of saying heated arguments) in the horticultural trade about which species of oregano is best or even available in seed form. There seems to be a complete mixing of species and seed sources and there are no real guarantees of which species you'll get.

PARSLEY

Parsley is one of the most famous of herbs, full of vitamins and even reputed to cure bad breath after you've eaten garlic. It's one of the main culinary herbs for summer growing and no summer salad is complete without it. You're going to read reports that parsley is a perennial plant. The truth of it is that it is a biennial, growing in its first year and flowering (and then dying) in its second.

When to Plant

Plant indoors in mid-January to get a jump on the season. This will produce a good-sized plant for the Victoria Day Weekend.

Sow directly into the ground every week from the time dandelions start blooming. After two months, stop planting as they won't have time to grow.

Where to Plant

Parsley prefers full sun to very light shade. Choose a well-drained soil that is not too alkaline (don't place any wood ashes around this plant). Parsley doesn't overwinter well in clay.

How to Plant

Plant seed .6 cm deep and firm the soil over top of the barely covered seed.

Indoors or directly sown in the garden, plant it so there's about 1 cm between seeds.

Care & Maintenance

Indoor culture means transplanting each seedling into its own pot when the seedling has four true leaves.

Outdoors, the seedlings should be thinned to 8 to 10 cm between plants when the seedlings have four true leaves. The thinnings can be eaten.

Additional Information

Harvest the outer leaves, allowing the inner bud to continue producing new tender growth.

In the fall, a few plants can be dug up, potted into large enough pots to contain the roots without chopping them back too much, and grown on a cool, sunny windowsill. The leaves can be harvested right until the plant starts to run out of energy. There's little point in trying to keep parsley alive after it stops producing leaves and wants to go dormant. You won't get a lot of leaves from it from this point on so discard it to the compost pile.

Outside plants that were sown very late in the fall will start growing as soon as spring starts. You can harvest them until they want to start throwing flowers. (They'll start producing really tall shoots and we call this "bolting.") By the time the overwintered plants have stopped producing new shoots, the new crop should be very close to producing. So your time without parsley will not be very long. Dig up any overwintered and nonproducing plants, compost them, and rely on the new crop.

ROSEMARY

Rosemary is one of the more famous herbs but is not used as much as other herbs because of its potent flavour. But, it's easy to grow in full sun. You should consider it a very tender shrub rather than a perennial.

When to Plant

Sow seeds indoors in January in order to have a large, 10-cm pot by May. Or sow outside in late May for a very late plant in September. Rosemary is a slow grower.

Where to Plant

Plant in full sun. Plant rosemary in the ground if you only want a single year from this plant; otherwise, pot it up and grow as a houseplant during the winter.

How to Plant

Sow seeds just below soil line—barely covering them—and keep soil temperature at 18°C minimum. They take a long time (30 days) to germinate and then they grow quite slowly for several months.

Tender tip cuttings root easily if you don't have any luck with seeding.

Rosemary prefers a warm soil over cool, and overwatering will kill seedlings.

Care & Maintenance

Rosemary might survive in Victoria if it's left outside year-round, but it will survive nowhere else in the country that has what we refer to as "winter." It's a tender shrub—very tender.

I grow mine in large pots and bring them indoors for the winter months. I find if I don't let them dry out completely, they grow much better than if they're allowed to dry out or watered in a roller-coaster style. I have an upright variety and a trailing variety in one pot so I get an "interesting" plant shape.

I prune the upright variety into a tree by removing all its bottom branches and shaping the top into whatever form I want with thin wires or stakes. You can easily shape and prune rosemary because it regrows quickly and forgives mistakes willingly.

Additional Information

Use this herb sparingly because it has quite a powerful taste. The flowers on rosemary typically bloom in early spring and can be hues of white through purple; there are even some pink tones.

My best bit of advice is that rosemary will grow straggly and look very ugly unless you are brutal with the pruning shears. Cut it back just when it starts to look ugly and don't worry because it will immediately start to grow back. This ability to regrow is one reason it makes such a good (and quick) topiary plant.

SAGE

Sage is a tough perennial plant in nearly all parts of Canada up to zone 3, where it becomes marginal. Once it's established, this plant will self-sow to give you all the sage you can possibly use for your Christmas turkey. It is an attractive plant as well, and can easily be tucked into the perennial border to provide a few leaves to harvest when you need them.

When to Plant

Plant in late January or mid-February in order to have a large plant by mid-May. Or, sow outdoors along with other late spring crops in early May in zone 4. Plant earlier in warmer areas and later by a week or two in colder zones.

Where to Plant

Plant in full sun to light shade. You can grow sage in almost any light level except full shade, but it flowers best in full sun if you're looking for an ornamental garden effect in addition to having an edible herb.

How to Plant

Sow seeds .6 cm deep, cover, and firm the soil over the seed. This depth should be just *barely* below the soil. Soil temperatures in the 20°C range germinate this seed quickly. Once the plant has developed four true leaves, grow it in a cooler spot (15°C) to keep the plant stocky. This may mean transplanting to a cooler spot.

Care & Maintenance

The best-tasting leaves are harvested right before the plant flowers. They are their most tender at this time.

This is a short-lived plant, in the order of 2 to 3 years, so you really want to encourage new seedlings every year to bring a new plant along to replace the old ones.

Older plants do tend to get a bit "woody" and are hard to make into an attractive plant. I tend to rip sage plants out when they start developing bare spots on the bottom stems. You can prune them in the spring (if the top growth has survived winter) to shape them and encourage new growth.

Additional Information

The Latin name for sage is *Salvia* and this means "to heal." Over the years, this herb has been recommended for almost every major disease known to humans. Indeed, it does have some medicinal properties including some related to Alzheimer's disease.

Some of the hybrid varieties are not overly hardy in a zone 5 garden. I've had poor luck, for example, trying to overwinter the variegated varieties such as 'Tricolor'.

SORREL

Sorrel gives a wonderful sour-apple taste to salads, and French chefs use it as a base herb for some tasty soups. It is easy to grow.

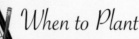

When to Plant

Planting from seed indoors in mid-March is best to get it well established before summer. It only takes 60 days from seed to harvest, so starting it ahead of time will give you an excellent addition to spring salads.

Sow outdoors along with radish and spinach as soon as you can get into the garden to plant.

Where to Plant

Sorrel does best in part shade with adequate water. I have grown it in full sun and it does fine as long as you don't let it dry out. Grow in any well-drained soil that is moderately rich in fertility.

How to Plant

Do not cover seed; simply lay them on the soil and press them down lightly so they are in contact with the soil. Water with lukewarm water. Seed will germinate in 7 to 10 days if you keep the soil temperature at 18°C and will take a few days longer if the soil is cooler.

Care & Maintenance

You can grow this plant as an annual or perennial. The difference is that with a perennial, you need to stop harvesting leaves in early to midsummer to allow the roots to develop strength so it will overwinter.

I generally have more than one plant going so I can harvest the outer leaves from one or two and let them die (so the plants function as annuals). I maintain one or two as perennials to give very early zest to spring salads.

Divide overwintered plants in early spring to increase the number of plants you want for the coming season.

Additional Information

If the sorrel plant develops seed stalks, cut them off to keep the leaves growing. If you let the seeds develop, leaf production will stop. Mind you, it will start again in the cool temperatures of fall whether you cut them off or not.

If you are really a berserker gardener and love sorrel, you could sow seeds every two weeks from early spring right through to early fall and have a continuous supply of fresh, tender leaves. You could then harvest an entire plant rather than just take a few leaves off the side of each. But that's serious sorrel gardening.

SPEARMINT

The entire mint family is easy to grow but comes with a very clear "plant thug" warning. This plant is the Genghis Khan of the plant world and never met a garden it didn't want to own.

When to Plant

Sow seed indoors in mid-March or outdoors in early spring when you're planting your spinach.

Where to Plant

Spearmint prefers full sun to part shade. This plant will survive in almost any soil. It does best in slightly damp soils in cool areas. In other words, this is one herb that doesn't love a hot, dry location.

How to Plant

Soil temperatures around 18°C are perfect for fast germination. Barely cover the seed and firm the soil over top of it. Spearmint doesn't want too high a temperature. Seedlings take about ten days to appear.

Otherwise, simply put a purchased plant in the ground and stand back. Water for the first week or two and the plant should be fine.

Spearmint is an easy plant to divide in the spring (anything with a bit of root or a node on a root will grow) and roots very easily from tip cuttings. Shove cuttings in a glass of water for quick and easy results.

Care & Maintenance

If you really want high production, water spearmint at least weekly and cut it regularly. It will respond with increased production. This advice holds true for all the mints available through garden centres and herb stores.

Additional Information

Every beginning gardener says one of two things (and sometimes both): "How bad can it really be?" and "Oh, I'll control it every spring." These are two stories we tell ourselves and here's the deal. Spearmint is a very fast-moving plant and it really will take over your garden either by seed or by underground rhizomes (shoots). The story we tell ourselves—"I'll control it"—is often waylaid by the best-laid plans of mice and gardeners. Not to mention that if you miss the smallest bit of root while digging, the entire plant will spring up from that tiny bit. Also, the seeds germinate fairly easily in almost all parts of the country (except maybe the far, far North) and it produces thousands of seedlings.

You've been warned.

I grow my spearmint in buckets. I remove the bottom of a bucket, sink it in the ground so the lip is 10 cm above the soil, and I allow the mint to live within the confines of the bucket. I prune off all flowering stems as soon as I see them. The suckers will try to escape over top of the lip, but I prune those off as well.

THYME

This is one of the most popular herbs in the garden because of its ease of growth, its toughness, and the wonderful varieties available. Let me tell you that this herb holds its flavour better when dried than almost any other herb. Even though it is used in many of the world's major cuisines, it can quickly overpower other herbs; use it with a light touch.

When to Plant

Sow seeds outdoors in early June or indoors about eight weeks before you want to put transplants outside.

Where to Plant

Plant in full sun in a well-drained soil. This plant will winterkill if it's left in clay soils or standing water. Put it in your hottest, sunniest spot where there is no standing water and only poor soil. In short, grow it in the hottest and worst soil you have.

How to Plant

Sow seed, press into the soil, and *barely* cover the seed. Other gardening books will suggest you cover them but all you really need to do is keep the seeds damp. This is a tiny seed and if you bury it deeply, you won't see it again, nor a plant. Germinate at 21°C soil temperatures and you should see plants in ten days.

The major problem home gardeners create for themselves is crowding the seedlings. If thyme is crowded, it rots quickly. Spread the seed at least .5 cm apart when planting; if you make a mistake, simply thin them to .5

to 1 cm when the plants have 4 true leaves. Mature plants should go into the garden roughly 25 cm apart. They'll quickly fill any intervening spaces.

Care & Maintenance

Harvest young growth regularly until you have enough for your needs. Then allow the plant to develop during the main part of the summer so it will store energy to survive the winter.

I've often seen a recommendation to "mulch" thyme plants for winter protection. My experience is that a mulch holds moisture around the stems and roots of this woody plant and kills it. I've had great luck growing it in a rock garden with a stone mulch that keeps moisture *away* from the plant, only giving it to the roots. So, I don't mulch.

Additional Information

Clip thyme back after it flowers to thicken it up and provide even more tender cuttings for the table. Only harvest tender shoots if you need extra thyme; otherwise, leave the new shoots to grow, mature, and make a bigger, stronger plant.

Index

Meet Doug

Doug Green has been in the nursery and greenhouse business most of his working life, running his own specialty plant nursery for more than twenty years. Doug jokingly states that he "learned a little bit about plants in the process." Over the years his gardens have included literally hundreds of varieties of vegetables including nearly fifty varieties of heritage tomatoes he grew for seed collecting for his nursery.

Doug has written seven books including a major award-winner that received the top prize for writing from the Garden Writers Association and a Canada Council grant. Doug writes a gardening column, is a radio show host, runs a gardening website answering gardening questions (www.simplegiftsfarm.com), blogs (http://blog.douggreensgarden.com), writes ebooks, gives free seminars, and generally has as much fun as possible. He can even be found on Twitter@DougGreen.

Green lives, gardens, and writes from an island in the 1000 Islands region of Lake Ontario where he and his partner (an acknowledged heirloom plant expert) are developing a garden together named "Someday" because this is the garden they both wanted to have "someday." If Doug isn't in the garden, he can be found sailing one of his old wooden boats or driving the countryside in his vintage English sports car.